GW00537740

BOOKWORMS

BERNARD FARRELL

MERCIER PRESS
IRISH PUBLISHER – IRISH STORY

MERCIER PRESS
Cork
www.mercierpress.ie

© Bernard Farrell, 2012

The moral right of Bernard Farrell to be identified
as the author of this work has been asserted.

ISBN: 978 1 85635 993 1

10 9 8 7 6 5 4 3 2 1

A CIP record for this title is available from the British Library

Bookworms is a copyright play and may not be performed without a licence.
All rights whatsoever in this play is strictly reserved and application for
performance etc. must be made before rehearsals start to Rosica Colin Ltd,
1 Clareville Grove Mews, London SW7 5AH. No performance may be given
unless a licence has been obtained.

All characters, locations and events in this book are entirely fictional.
Any resemblance to any person, living or dead, which may occur inadvertently
is completely unintentional.

This book is sold subject to the condition that it shall not, by way of trade
or otherwise, be lent, resold, hired out or otherwise circulated without the
publisher's prior consent in any form of binding or cover other than that in which
it is published and without a similar condition including this condition being
imposed on the subsequent purchaser.

No part of this publication may be reproduced or transmitted in any form or by
any means, electronic or mechanical, including photocopying, recording or any
information or retrieval system, without the prior permission
of the publisher in writing.

Typeset by Dominic Carroll, Ardfield, Co. Cork
Printed and bound in the EU.

For Gloria

This play was first presented at the Abbey Theatre, Dublin, on 1 June 2010, with the following cast:

Ann (40)	Marion O'Dwyer
Larry (50)	Phelim Drew
Aisling (18)	Liz Fitzgibbon
Dorothy (60s)	Deirdre Donnelly
Robert (45)	Louis Lovett
Jennifer (30s)	Karen Egan
Vincent (50s)	Michael Glenn Murphy

Director	Jim Culleton
Designer	Anthony Lamble
Lighting	Kevin McFadden

Act 1

The drawing room of Larry and Ann's suburban home.

In stage-right wall are glass doors to a newly built conservatory, off. In the back wall, at stage right, is a large, built-in, plasma TV screen. Beneath it, a desk on which stands a computer. Further left in the back wall is the entrance door to the room. In stage-left wall, a door to what is referred to as 'the library'.

The room is tastefully and comfortably furnished. A house phone is prominently placed.

It is an early autumn evening, about 7.30, the evening of Ann's Book Club meeting.

The house phone is ringing. Establish. Then Ann comes through the entrance door, carrying wine, cheese and crackers. She is forty, attractive, somewhat insecure, but determined. Now she is nervous about the evening and clearly agitated by the ringing phone.

ANN   (CALLS) Larry, can you get that? (LOUDER) Larry?

                LARRY COMES IN THROUGH THE ENTRANCE DOOR. HE IS FIFTY, SOMEWHAT GRUFF, DOWN-TO-EARTH, BUT PLEASANT. HIS ARMS ARE FULL OF BOOKS. HE IS ALSO NERVOUS AND AGITATED.

LARRY   Ann, that phone's ringing.

ANN   I know. Will you get it?

LARRY   (ARMS FULL) Me?

ANN	Please, Larry! I don't want to hear someone else cancelling.
LARRY	Then let it ring.
ANN	But then I won't know if they are cancelling.
LARRY	But you just said you didn't want to know!
ANN	I said I didn't want to hear, not that I didn't want to know!
LARRY	Jesus Christ! (PICKS UP THE PHONE) Hello? Ah hello, Aisling. (TO ANN) It's Aisling.
ANN	(CONCERNED) Aisling? What's wrong?
LARRY	(INTO PHONE) Great to hear from you, love. How are you?
ANN	Is she all right? Is she?
LARRY	(INTO PHONE) What? No, it's not on. (TO ANN, ANXIOUSLY) Is the computer on?
ANN	What? No.
LARRY	(INTO PHONE) Oh, ok. Now? Ok. Is there a problem or …
ANN	(ANXIOUSLY) What is it?
LARRY	Ok, right away. Bye Aisling. (PUTS THE PHONE DOWN) It's Aisling – we're to turn on the computer quick, she's coming online to see us and talk to us again, on the Skype webcam thing.
ANN	Oh good God – did she say what's wrong?
LARRY	No! (AT THE COMPUTER) How's this it goes? (RAPIDLY PRESSING BUTTONS AND KEYS)
ANN	Leave it, leave it, I'll do it! (DOING IT) How did she sound?
LARRY	Like she was in Australia.
ANN	But she is in Australia!

LARRY	I know. That's how she sounded.
ANN	What did you press here? Why is nothing happening?
LARRY	I pressed nothing. Where's the book?
ANN	What book?
LARRY	The instruction book.
ANN	We haven't time for that.
LARRY	How did you do it last time? What did you press?
ANN	I know what to press if you'd just stop talking to me and let me do it!
	SUDDENLY, THE COMPUTER LIGHTS UP – HOMEPAGE ON SCREEN.
LARRY	There it is now. There it is! Don't touch anything!
ANN	But I have to get onto the site!
LARRY	Right – then get it up on the big screen like before.
ANN	(AT THE KEYBOARD) There it is. Now, name …
LARRY	Get it up on the big screen.
ANN	(AT THE COMPUTER) … password …
LARRY	Get it up on the big screen.
ANN	… wait for it to come up …
LARRY	Ann, get it up on the big screen.
ANN	Larry, what do you think I'm trying to do?
LARRY	All right. Keep going.
ANN	There!
	THE COMPUTER SKYPE LOGO TRANSFERS ONTO THE PLASMA TV SCREEN.

LARRY	That's it! It's there! Don't touch anything.
ANN	(STOPS) And now, Larry, listen carefully. When I press 'accept', Aisling will appear and we'll be on camera.
LARRY	Right – let's go!
ANN	No, it's not 'let's go'! We don't know if she's in some kind of trouble or not, so we have to appear calm and relaxed.
LARRY	(IMPATIENTLY) Right.
ANN	And, Book Club or no Book Club, we listen to her. She's not doing this for nothing, whatever time it is there.
LARRY	Right.
ANN	So we are calm and relaxed and not worried about anything.
LARRY	(ANXIOUSLY) Right! We're calm! Grand!
	A SUDDEN CALM POSE FROM BOTH, AS ANN HITS THE KEYS. ON THE TV SCREEN, AISLING APPEARS. SHE IS EIGHTEEN, NOW SLEEPY AND JUST OUT OF BED.
AISLING	There you are! Hi Mum!
ANN	(IN FRONT OF THE WEBCAM. VERY UPBEAT) Hello Aisling, love – how are you?
AISLING	Great, Mum – how are you, how's Dad, how's everything?
LARRY	(RELAXED) Hello Aisling – I'm great, relaxing here, as you can see.
ANN	(TO LARRY) She can't see – get in front of the camera.
LARRY	Where? (MOVES)
AISLING	(AMUSED) Ok – I can see you now, Dad.

LARRY	Oh grand. Yes, just relaxing here. What time is it there?
ANN	(QUIETLY TO LARRY) Never mind that!
AISLING	Five in the morning, Dad, but I was just awake thinking about you, and Mum and how things are …
LARRY	But everything is grand here, couldn't be better.
AISLING	Why, have you work coming in now?
LARRY	Aisling, I worked hard enough through the old Celtic Tiger to …
AISLING	So it's still the same.
ANN	Aisling, don't you be worrying – this recession will be over in no time – and really I don't know why you're out there, you should be here at college, you got your points and …
AISLING	Mum, not again!
ANN	Well, when *are* you coming home? I don't know why you had to go galloping off to …
AISLING	(IRRITATED) It's my gap year – that's fifty-two weeks – and there's three gone!
ANN	Yes, and you're there on your own when you could be …
AISLING	For God's sake! I didn't ring you for this!
ANN	Why, is there something else wrong?
AISLING	There's nothing wrong – but this is your first Book Club there, and the first with men! – and I was just wondering how it's going, like who's coming over and all that, that's all.
ANN	(CALMER) Oh, it's going great – some can't make it but most are coming, the first should be here very soon and …

AISLING	And what men, like what husbands, are coming?
ANN	Well, your father will be sitting in for one book, my choice, the Harper Lee one ...
LARRY	... and then I'm leaving them to it, Aisling.
AISLING	Oh Dad, I think it's great you're doing that, meeting people again.
LARRY	Aisling, I meet people all the time.
AISLING	And Mum, who else is coming?
ANN	Well, Jennifer Travers, of course, and her husband Robert, from the bank ...
AISLING	Oh I didn't think Mr Travers would come ...
ANN	Oh yes, very enthusiastic ... and Sandra and her partner Michael ...
LARRY	And old Dorothy will be here ...
ANN	... and Marian and Trevor, and I think that's it.
AISLING	Oh, that's a nice crowd.
	SUDDENLY, A MALE SHOUT FROM THE BACKGROUND TO AISLING, ON SCREEN.
AISLING	(TO OFF, MERRILY) Get out and shut the door – I'm talking to my parents.
ANN	Who's that, Aisling, who's there with you?
AISLING	Just some friends, Mum. (TO OFF) Out, now! All of you!
MALE VOICE	(MERRILY) We love her, Mrs Aisling! She's a great ride!
AISLING	(MERRILY) Shut up! Out, now! (TO CAMERA AGAIN) Sorry about that, Mum. They're gone.
ANN	(CONCERNED) Who are they, Aisling? Where are you staying?
AISLING	Just some people I met here – (TRYING) that

	last guy, he has a motorbike, that's what he was saying, he'll give me a ride on it in the morning.
LARRY	Well, you make sure you wear a crash helmet, Aisling.
ANN	(TO LARRY) For God's sake! (TO CAMERA) Aisling, I hope you are with nice people.
AISLING	I am, I am! I have to go soon – but I wanted to ask you about Uncle Vincent. Is he still there?
ANN	Vincent? Yes love, he's still here. Don't you be worrying about Uncle Vincent.
LARRY	You're not thinking about the budgie, are you?
	ANN SHOOTS LARRY A LOOK.
AISLING	No, of course not – but he won't be coming down to the Book Club, will he? I mean when Mr Travers and all the husbands are there?
ANN	No love, why would he? He'll be upstairs working on his projects. Why do you ask?
AISLING	No reason, Mum, that's cool. Listen, I have to go now …
ANN	Is that all you wanted?
AISLING	Yes, just thinking about you all. Look, you're on broadband so just leave the computer on this site – don't close it down and it will go to snooze – in case I want to get in touch with you again when I wake up.
ANN	All right, love.
AISLING	But I will phone first and you just move the mouse and we'll connect, ok?
ANN	All right, Aisling. And I really wish you were here …
AISLING	Yeah sure, Mum. And good luck at the Book

Club, Dad.

LARRY   Do my best, Aisling.

AISLING   Bye Mum. Bye Dad. Love you. (MERRILY
          SHOUTS TO OFF) God's sake – I'm coming!

          AISLING IS GONE. THE SCREEN SHOWS THE
          WEBCAM SITE … AND WILL SOON GO TO BLACK.
          ANN GOES BACK TO HER PREPARATIONS, AS:

ANN   The sooner she's home and off to college the
          better. Her and her gap year. And she wanted
          to say more – I know she did. She's not ready
          for that life. And why did you have to mention
          the budgie to her?

LARRY   I thought it might be playing on her mind.

          THERE IS A TIMID, CAUTIOUS KNOCK ON THE
          ENTRANCE DOOR.

ANN   What's that?

LARRY   Must be Vincent with more books.

ANN   Tell him not to bring any down while they're
          all here.

          LARRY OPENS THE DOOR AND LOOKS OUTSIDE.

LARRY   (TO OFF) Ah, Vincent, more? Great. Thanks
          very much.

ANN   (CALLS) Thank you, Vincent. I think that's
          enough now.

LARRY   (TAKING BOOKS FROM VINCENT, OFF) I think
          that's plenty now and we hope you won't be
          disturbed by any noise down here. (LISTENS
          TO A SOFT VOICE, OFF) Grand. Thanks again,
          Vincent. And good luck with your cathedral in
          Spain.

          LARRY CLOSES THE DOOR. HE NOW HOLDS TEN
          MORE BOOKS.

LARRY	He's gone back up. Will I put these around here or where?
ANN	It's just chat and finger-food in here – our Book Club proper will be in the library.
LARRY	Oh right. (GOING)
ANN	No, wait. What are they anyway?
LARRY	They're all good stuff. Look – *Treasure Island*.
ANN	(TAKES IT) Well that's out for a start.
LARRY	That's a great book, Ann.
ANN	Not to Jennifer. (CHECKING THE BOOKS) *Anne of Green Gables* – that's all right. Never heard of that, but lovely cover. Good God – Danielle Steele! (REMOVES IT) Milan Kundera, Vassily Grossman, Günter Grass – they all sound great – Waugh, O'Connor, Lavin, grand. No paperbacks. (REMOVES THESE) Yes, Zoë Heller, they love her. Ok, all the rest are fine, all in. Don't leave the others lying around.
LARRY	Right. (A PHONE RINGS) I think that's your mobile.
ANN	(FINDS IT AND CHECKS IT) Marian! Well, I'm letting that ring – I've had enough bad news already.
LARRY	Right. (GOES INTO THE LIBRARY)
	ANN CONTINUES TO PREPARE THE ROOM. THE MOBILE CONTINUES TO RING.
ANN	(ANGRILY) All right! (INTO PHONE, SWEETLY) Hello? Ah, Marian. (LISTENS) Oh, what a shame. (LISTENS) Oh you poor thing. But maybe Trevor can come anyway …? (LISTENS) Oh I see. Shame. Yes, I'll tell Jennifer. Bye, Marian. (CLOSES PHONE) Yes, but you turned up for all the other ones!

ANN   I answered it. She's not coming either. Or Trevor.

LARRY   That's a pity.

ANN   It's a disaster.

LARRY   No it's not – there's still Jennifer and Robert … and Sandra and Michael and old Dorothy and me.

ANN   Less than we ever had, even with husbands. So Larry, please, could you not sit in for the *two* books, just to make up the numbers?

LARRY   Oh no way, Ann – I'm only going to *your* book because I saw Gregory Peck in the film.

ANN   Yes, but then you read most of it …

LARRY   … and that was grand – but this other book, the one Jennifer picked, even you said that was a load of shite.

ANN   I did not say that! I said it was heavy going!

LARRY   Exactly, and I'm not having her looking down her nose at me …

ANN   She won't be!

LARRY   And that husband of hers hates my guts …

ANN   He doesn't! And this is a great opportunity for you to meet him casually …

LARRY   Except I don't want to meet him casually or any other way – him and his bank have me over a barrel and he knows it – and I know nothing about the book – I never even heard of Veronica Woolf …

ANN   Virginia Woolf – but you can do what I did – I just Googled it up on the computer, got a few quotes and the general idea, and …

LARRY	(DETERMINED) I'm not doing it, Ann. I'll be found out.
ANN	You won't – and we'll be doing Jennifer's book second so you'll have time to get Vincent to Google it up for you …
LARRY	No, Ann, no!
	THE DOORBELL RINGS.
ANN	That's probably them now. (HURRIES TO THE WINDOW) Say you'll do it, Larry, please – just do this for me.
LARRY	(WEAKENING) Ann, for Christ sake – I'm not a book reader.
ANN	(LOOKING OUT) It's all right – it's only Dorothy, in another new car, the size of it. Will you let her in before she rings again – and Larry, let's try to show everyone that, recession or no recession, we are contented, confident and happy – and that this evening is going to be fun.
LARRY	Fun?
ANN	Oh and don't forget: poor Dorothy's sister died since our last meeting and it's not long since her cousin, who was in Bolivia, suddenly dropped dead.
LARRY	Jaysus, that should liven up the evening all right.
	LARRY GOES. ANN ANXIOUSLY MAKES LAST-MINUTE PREPARATIONS. THEN LARRY LEADS IN DOROTHY: A REFINED LADY IN HER MID-SIXTIES.
DOROTHY	(TO LARRY) Well, it is a credit to you.
LARRY	Thank you, Dorothy – and here's your hostess for the evening.

ANN   Welcome, Dorothy, welcome. (HUGS)

DOROTHY   Thank you, Ann – your house is so lovely.

ANN   Can't have a builder and not use him! There'll
           be a full tour as soon as the others arrive.

DOROTHY   Oh that reminds me – I met Sandra this after-
           noon and she won't be able to be with us, or
           her Michael.

ANN   Oh.

DOROTHY   Something about taking their second-youngest
           to badminton.

ANN   That means we are now down to Jennifer and
           Robert and you and me.

DOROTHY   Well, some non-respondents may turn up, that
           frequently happens.

ANN   That's true – and I think Larry may join us for
           the two books.

DOROTHY   Oh very good – you're most welcome, Larry.

LARRY   Well I haven't fully decided …

ANN   So hopefully now, it'll all go well. Please sit,
           Dorothy. And I have set out some wine and
           cheese and crackers …

DOROTHY   (HUNGRILY) Oh lovely. (REACHES FOR A
           CRACKER)

ANN   (STERNLY) … that we can all have as soon as
           Jennifer and Robert arrive.

DOROTHY   (RETREATS FROM THE CRACKERS) Of course.

ANN   And then, after food, we will be having
           our meeting proper in our library, there,
           all carpeted, soundproofed, with concealed
           lighting and separate desk lights.

DOROTHY   (TO LARRY) And did you …?

ANN	Oh yes, all designed and built by Larry. And Larry, do you want to go upstairs now?
LARRY	Pardon?
ANN	Didn't you want to check something before our Book Club starts – and Dorothy, perhaps if we discuss the Harper Lee book first, then a break for refreshments, and then the Virginia Woolf second?
DOROTHY	Of course, if that is what is agreed.
ANN	Grand. (TO LARRY) So you can go up and …
LARRY	(GOING) Well yes, but I haven't fully decided …
ANN	(A REMINDER) And Larry! (LARRY STOPS) Dorothy, you know how sad Larry and I were to hear of your recent bereavement.
LARRY	Oh yes, your cousin – our sincere condolences.
ANN	(POINTED) And more recently, your sister.
LARRY	Oh yes, and more recently, your sister, but first, your cousin.
DOROTHY	Yes – very kind of both of you. Thank you very much.
LARRY	(TRYING) I believe he was in Bosnia when he suddenly died.
DOROTHY	Who was?
LARRY	Your cousin.
ANN	(CORRECTING) No, in Bolivia!
DOROTHY	Yes, in Bolivia, and …
LARRY	Oh, Bolivia? And he lived there, did he?
DOROTHY	No, just suddenly died there – and, to clarify, he was actually a she and she had been living in Argentina but died while in Bolivia.

LARRY	Oh I see. And he was really a she, was he? – I mean, was he always a she or did he just suddenly decide …?
ANN	(ANNOYED) Larry, Dorothy's cousin was a woman and I told you that and that she died in Bolivia, I told you that too.
LARRY	Yes yes, sorry, I understand, so always a she, a woman – and our condolences again, Dorothy – so many bereavements in such a short time.
DOROTHY	Yes – and then, only two weeks ago, my chiro-practor, who was a dear and loyal friend, also died.
ANN	Oh Dorothy, I didn't hear that. That's very sad.
LARRY	And was he a she or a he?
DOROTHY	My chiropractor was a man. He lived in Manorhamilton but was, in fact, Swedish.
LARRY	Ah, a Swedish man. Our deepest condolences again, Dorothy, at this sad time for you.
DOROTHY	And for all of us really. Wasn't it the wonderful E.M. Forster who described each of us as 'a tiny night-light, suffocating in its own wax, always on the point of expiring'.
ANN	(LOST) It was indeed.
LARRY	(LOST) Absolutely.
ANN	And now, Larry, before the others arrive …
LARRY	(ESCAPING) Yes yes – just a few things to do, Dorothy, if you'll excuse me.
DOROTHY	Of course, Larry.
ANN	(A HINT) To the Lighthouse.
LARRY	What? Oh right.
	LARRY GOES. ANN AND DOROTHY NOW MORE RELAXED.

14

ANN	Now Dorothy, what will you have?
DOROTHY	(HUNGRILY) Oh, let me see. (REACHES FOR THE CRACKERS)
ANN	(WITH THE BOTTLES) Red or white?
DOROTHY	(REALISES. ABANDONS THE CRACKERS) Oh, just water please – I'm driving.
ANN	(MERRILY) And I'm not. (POURING) So why not. And water for you. I think it was Pellegrino you like, if I remember right. (POURS)
DOROTHY	How nice of you to remember that – yes, I acquired a taste for that when we lived in Italy, in the Lombardy region. (TAKES HER GLASS) Thank you so much and best wishes for tonight.
ANN	Oh thank you, Dorothy – cheers.
	THEY DRINK – ANN WITH SOME ENTHUSIASM. THEN:
DOROTHY	I am almost afraid to ask, but how is he? (POINTS UPSTAIRS)
ANN	(CONFIDENTIALLY) Well, it's not the Celtic Tiger anymore: sometimes all he can talk about is machinery rusting on sites, bank repayments, letting people go – maybe it got to Aisling, sometimes it gets to me (INDICATES HER GLASS) – but I always say, it can't last, and it can't – so hopefully.
DOROTHY	Indeed. But I was actually asking about his brother.
ANN	(STOPS) Pardon?
DOROTHY	His brother – Vincent, isn't it? I sometimes see him walking down to buy his paper and sometimes walking back *with* his paper – but I always remember what you told me about him,

in confidence of course, after our last Book Club, at Monica's.

ANN   At Monica's?

DOROTHY   After it, in my car, because you didn't take your car that evening.

ANN   (EVADING) Oh and would you blame me? I know Monica, pouring the drinks non-stop, topping everyone up without anyone noticing!

DOROTHY   Yes, I just had water that evening and then I drove you home and that's when you told me, about Vincent.

ANN   (EMBARRASSED) Do you know, Dorothy, I remember so little about that drive home.

DOROTHY   Oh nothing to remember really – but you did mention about Vincent and about the budgie.

ANN   (STOPS) The budgie? I didn't think I …

DOROTHY   How Aisling was cleaning out the budgie's cage and Vincent was holding the budgie in his hand and then they began to argue about something, Aisling and Vincent, and Vincent suddenly … (CLOSES HER FIST)

ANN   What? No no, well yes, yes, that is true, but it was all an accident, a complete accident …

DOROTHY   Of course because we all know how incredibly gentle he is with his hands – that church that he built, the one in the newsagent's window …

ANN   Yes, yes …

DOROTHY   Is it with 150,000 matchsticks?

ANN   Yes, something like that …

DOROTHY   Well that shows great gentleness.

ANN   (ANXIOUS) Yes, but I have absolutely no recollection of …

DOROTHY   Well, not that it matters – I was just wonder-
          ing if he is still staying here?

ANN   Well yes, for the time being ... upstairs ... but
          he won't be coming down or disturbing us ...

DOROTHY   Oh I wouldn't object to meeting him.

ANN   Well, he likes to be left alone most of the time
          – and I still cannot believe I said anything
          about the ...

DOROTHY   Oh it was just a comment you made on the
          way home from Monica's and all in absolute
          confidence of course.

ANN   Of course. I just don't remember saying it.
          (ANXIOUSLY DRINKS)

          A SOUND OUTSIDE. TYRES ON GRAVEL.

ANN   Oh my God – is that a car? (HURRIES TO
          THE WINDOW) It's them! Larry will hate his
          gravel being kicked up like that. (NERVOUSLY
          PEEPING) Here they come. I'll let them ring.
          (PAUSE) Which should be any minute.

DOROTHY   Don't worry, Ann – I'm sure it will be a very
          successful evening.

ANN   I hope so. (LIGHTLY) Or I may get detention
          from Jennifer.

DOROTHY   (LIGHTLY) Once a teacher.

          THE DOORBELL RINGS.

ANN   That's it now. All set. Here we go.

          ANN GOES. DOROTHY IMMEDIATELY, AND
          HUNGRILY, PICKS UP A CRACKER. SHE IS ABOUT
          TO EAT IT, CONSIDERS BEING CAUGHT AS
          VOICES ARE HEARD OUTSIDE, QUICKLY PUTS IT
          BACK, ALL AS:

JENNIFER (OFF) No no, perfect directions, Ann.

ROBERT	(OFF) Yes, absolutely spot on.
ANN	(OFF) Oh good.
JENNIFER	(OFF) Although that last signpost does have a tree growing across it.
ANN	(OFF) Oh yes, they should cut that.
	ANN LEADS IN JENNIFER AND ROBERT. JENNIFER IS IN HER THIRTIES, CONFIDENT AND ENERGETIC. ROBERT IS FORTY-FIVE, A SOCIABLE, ASSURED MAN.
ANN	(COMING IN) Now, here we are.
JENNIFER	(ENTHUSIASTIC) Dorothy! I just knew you'd be here. (HUGS)
DOROTHY	Hello, Jennifer.
ROBERT	(MERRILY) Yes, she knew because your car's parked outside.
JENNIFER	(LIGHTLY) No, because Dorothy is absolutely dependable, Mr Smarty Pants.
ROBERT	Lovely to see you, Dorothy.
DOROTHY	Hello Robert.
ROBERT	Am I right in saying that you two have a one-hundred-per-cent attendance record at these Book Clubs?
DOROTHY	I think we have.
ANN	Yes, we have!
ROBERT	(MERRILY) Gold stars for the top girls in Jennifer's class.
JENNIFER	(LIGHTLY) And no alpha-dog behaviour tonight, Robert, please – remember you are now in the last bastion of female exclusivity: a Book Club.
DOROTHY	(MERRILY) Yes!

ROBERT	But not alone – I have Larry and Trevor and Michael as back-up!
ANN	Bad news everyone: Marian and Trevor won't be coming …
DOROTHY	And Sandra said she and Michael cannot attend.
JENNIFER	(ANNOYED) Oh for Heaven's sake! Well I hope they all sent in their reports and opinions on our two books?
DOROTHY	Not to me.
ANN	Not to here.
JENNIFER	But I thought we all agreed that if we cannot attend, we would ensure that our written contributions would be here and, ideally, circulated? Oh never mind.
ROBERT	But Larry is Ok, isn't he?
ANN	Yes, and down in a moment, Robert. Now, what would everybody like?
JENNIFER	(OF THE WINE) Oh my goodness, do I see a Te Tera Sauvignon 2007?
ANN	(PROUDLY) Yes, I remembered. You'll have some?
JENNIFER	Oh yes, please. Oh and Gorgonzola – *la reine de fromage*! I think I'm going to enjoy this evening.
ANN	(POURING) I hope so. And Brie and cheddar there too. And Dorothy is on water.
DOROTHY	Yes, driving tonight.
JENNIFER	(MERRILY) Take note, Robert.
ROBERT	I am. Red please, Ann. 'Everything in moderation – and moderation in moderation'.
ANN	Very good, Robert.

JENNIFER	And your house is lovely, Ann.
ANN	Thank you – we'll have our little tour soon.
JENNIFER	Well, if we have time – a lot to squeeze in this evening.
ANN	Of course – and we'll have our two Book Club sessions in our library. (EXPLAINS) That door there.
JENNIFER	Oh excellent.
ROBERT	And did we all enjoy the books or is there revolution in the air?
JENNIFER	(EATING) The one question you should not ask, Robert.
ANN	Not at the cheese-and-wine stage, Robert.
JENNIFER	All reaction should be reserved for the inner sanctum.
ANN	Yes, and our library is completely sound-proofed …
JENNIFER	Fantastic, so not a word before. Although I am very excited about some interesting details that I and my sixth-years unearthed about Virginia Woolf's private life which, *entre nous*, may give us a somewhat new perspective on her fiction.
ANN	Oh, that sounds intriguing, Jennifer.
DOROTHY	I have always been most interested in how her relationships informed her fiction in ways that …
JENNIFER	But please, ladies, and Robert, all for later.
	THE DOOR OPENS AND LARRY COMES IN. HE IS CLEARLY ANXIOUS, BUT IS TRYING HARD TO APPEAR ASSURED.
LARRY	Good evening, everybody.

ROBERT	Ah, reinforcements.
LARRY	(GREETING) Jennifer!
JENNIFER	Larry!
LARRY	Long time no see.
JENNIFER	Yes, but aren't you looking well.
LARRY	And why not. And Robert. It's Men United tonight.
ROBERT	United we stand, divided we crawl.
JENNIFER	And Larry, we've been reading all about your brother in the local paper.
LARRY	Vincent? The matchstick churches? Yes, we're all proud of that.
DOROTHY	I saw the model in the newsagent.
JENNIFER	Is it fifty thousand matchsticks?
DOROTHY	One hundred and fifty thousand!
JENNIFER	Goodness me.
ANN	The paper said it's like brain surgery.
ROBERT	Absolutely.
JENNIFER	And is he still here?
ANN	Yes, for a little while more.
LARRY	But I doubt if he'll be down.
ANN	He needs the solitude.
JENNIFER	Oh, of course.
ROBERT	And the concentration.
LARRY	Exactly, so I don't think he'll be down. (QUIETLY TO ANN) Printed off one page for me. (TRIES TO SHOW HER A PAGE FROM HIS POCKET – GREEN, A4 TYPING PAPER)
ANN	(IGNORING THIS. LOUDLY) Red or white, Larry?

LARRY	What?
ANN	The wine.
LARRY	(PUTS THE PAGE AWAY QUICKLY) Oh red. No, white. No, red. (THEN) Give me a beer, will you.
ROBERT	(MERRILY) Excellent choice, Larry – eventually!
LARRY	Absolutely. (AWKWARDLY) And Dorothy – you're all right there?
DOROTHY	Yes, thank you very much, Larry.
LARRY	No problem – and my sincere condolences again.
DOROTHY	Oh thank you, thank you.
LARRY	(AWKWARDLY TO JENNIFER AND ROBERT) You both know that Dorothy's sister died recently?
ANN	Yes Larry, I think they know.
JENNIFER	Yes, so sad, and before that, your cousin.
DOROTHY	Yes.
LARRY	(TO ROBERT) Who was, in fact, a woman.
ROBERT	Really? And was that only discovered after he died?
LARRY	No, he was, it seems, always a woman.
JENNIFER	I never thought she was anything else but a woman?
DOROTHY	Yes!
LARRY	Yes so you were absolutely right, Jennifer. But then, as if that wasn't enough for poor Dorothy, she has been telling us that she also lost her close friend, who lived in Manorhamilton but came from Sweden, a very dear and loyal friend that she knew at choir practise.

DOROTHY	What? No, that's not true, Larry.
LARRY	Oh, still alive, is he?
DOROTHY	No, he is dead ...
LARRY	He wasn't a woman, was he?
DOROTHY	No ...
JENNIFER	Dorothy, I never knew you were in a choir.
ROBERT	Hidden talents, eh?
DOROTHY	No, I never had anything to do with choirs.
JENNIFER	But the choir practise?
DOROTHY	No, Ingemar was my chiropractor, for my back trouble.
ANN	(ANNOYED TO LARRY) Dorothy said it was her chiropractor!
LARRY	Oh right.
DOROTHY	And he was simply wonderful, allowed me to do some gardening again – I used to visit him occasionally up in Manorhamilton, as a patient but also as a friend, and I was just about to visit him again when I heard the news.
JENNIFER	Goodness. And didn't you tell me that your dear sister died within twenty-four hours of you planning to visit her?
DOROTHY	Yes and she was in perfect health.
ANN	So tragic.
ROBERT	And did you also plan to visit your cousin before she ...?
DOROTHY	Oh no no, she didn't live in this country ...
LARRY	She was out in Bosnia.
ANN	Bulgaria.
DOROTHY	Bolivia, she was in Bolivia.

LARRY	Bolivia.
JENNIFER	So you hadn't planned to visit her?
DOROTHY	No but when she died, she was planning to visit me, and suddenly she was gone.
JENNIFER	Oh.
DOROTHY	So I never saw any of them, all my loyal friends, gone.
JENNIFER	Unbelievably tragic.
ANN	Yes. (PAUSE. NOW SUDDENLY LIVELY) And now, do we have time for a quick tour of all we have done …
JENNIFER	(ENTHUSIASTIC) Yes! Of course! Albeit an abbreviated one.
ANN	Five minutes, maximum.
DOROTHY	(STANDING) Yes, that would be nice.
ROBERT	If it's ok, Ann, I may skip the tour.
ANN	Of course, Robert – you can keep Larry company.
JENNIFER	But we want you guys to be ready when we return.
ROBERT	We will, don't worry, we will.
	AS THEY GO, DOROTHY PAUSES AT THE TABLE TO SURREPTITIOUSLY TAKE SOME CRACKERS. ALL NOTICE HER. SHE THEN NOTICES THEM.
DOROTHY	(APOLOGETICALLY) Perhaps just to nibble.
ANN	And why not. After you, Jennifer, and Dorothy … (AS THEY EXIT) … now the hallway where you came in: we decided to parquet the flooring, and we also set back this wall to give the hallway more space …
	DOOR CLOSES. THEY ARE GONE. ROBERT AND LARRY AWKWARDLY TOGETHER.

ROBERT	Wine is fantastic – but do I spy with my little eye something else beginning with 'W'?
LARRY	What? (SEES) Oh the whiskey? Of course, help yourself.
ROBERT	Cat's away the mice turn into rats. You too?
LARRY	No, I'm grand.
ROBERT	Just a splash for *moi*. (POURS A GLASS) And Dorothy, eh? (MERRILY) If I ever hear she's planning to visit me, I'll phone the undertaker right away.
LARRY	Yes. Amazing coincidences.
ROBERT	More to that than meets the eye.
LARRY	You think so?
ROBERT	I know so. Can't say much – but we handled her late-husband's estate and business interests and now hers, so enough said. But I can say this – although they never got on, hardly spoke to one another, he left her a wealthy widow. You know her house, all that land, that car outside?
LARRY	Oh yes.
ROBERT	And property abroad, and no kids? On the pig's back. If you weren't married, Larry, you could hang your hat up there and give the recession the fingers.
LARRY	(MERRILY) Or you could?
ROBERT	(MERRILY) Not so sure. You see that coming across the bedroom every night, you might begin to think: 'Jesus, is this worth it?'
LARRY	Good point.
ROBERT	But when she goes, someone will do well. Cats-and-dogs home probably. What did you think of the Woolf?

LARRY   The wolf? What wolf?

ROBERT   Virginia. The book. *To the Lighthouse*. Are
               we thinking the same thing about that book,
               Larry?

LARRY   (CONFIDENTLY) Oh yes, I think so. I just read
               the first bit and I thought it was the greatest
               … (load of rubbish)…

ROBERT   … work of art? Couldn't agree more. She was
               a groundbreaker, wasn't she? A genius. Kicked
               out all the literary rules with that one.

LARRY   (BACKTRACKING) What? Oh absolutely.

ROBERT   Absolutely. Groundbreaker and genius.

               ROBERT MOVES IDLY AROUND THE ROOM.
               LARRY TAKES THE OPPORTUNITY TO TAKE
               THE GREEN SHEET OF PRINTED PAPER FROM
               HIS POCKET AND QUICKLY READ IT. HE PUTS IT
               AWAY.

LARRY   (VERY INFORMED) Personally speaking, I'd
               say about Virginia Woolf that her novels are
               very experimental and they make her one of
               the foremost, modernist, literary figures of the
               twentieth century. That's what I think anyway.

ROBERT   Totally agree, Larry. I think we can take on
               the ladies with this one.

LARRY   Absolutely. But we're doing Ann's book first –
               that one comes later.

ROBERT   Perfect. (AWKWARD PAUSE) And while we're
               here, Larry, you and I, before they come back,
               we may as well mention the elephant.

LARRY   The elephant? What elephant?

ROBERT   In the room. Our loans, your non-repayments,
               all that – maybe you'd drop in for a chat some
               time?

LARRY	Oh of course, no problem.
ROBERT	(CASUALLY) It's just that all our phone calls, faxes, emails, even courier mails …
LARRY	I know – but I'm getting around to all that now.
ROBERT	And that's great, Larry, because nobody wants it all to get out of control, nobody wants it to go beyond our friendship and into the hands of the legal guys and suddenly you're up in the High Court for weeks on end with maybe costs against you and, worse-case scenario, maybe a custodial sentence and you selling off stuff and your family devastated and everyone suddenly wide-eyed, wondering how it ever got to this. Nobody wants that, Larry.
LARRY	No, of course not.
ROBERT	Least of all me, who sanctioned your loans in the first place …
LARRY	I know, I know …
ROBERT	… and had faith in you. So maybe you'd just drop in and see our guys …
LARRY	Oh I will, I will for certain.
ROBERT	Maybe early next week if you can – but now, no more about that, now it's the Book Club, and, if I'm not mistaken, here come the girls!
	ROBERT HIDES HIS WHISKEY GLASS AND HOLDS HIS WINE GLASS AS ANN, JENNIFER AND DOROTHY ENTER, ALL ENJOYING THEIR CHAT.
JENNIFER	(MERRILY) … and it was only then that she realised she had built it north-facing!
ANN	(MERRILY) Oh my God!
DOROTHY	(MERRILY) The poor thing!

JENNIFER	But I had warned her. Tour over, boys – and fantastic house, Larry.
LARRY	Oh thanks very much.
JENNIFER	But now, all set? We have a lot to do and we are way behind time ... so I think we should crack on at once ... (TOWARDS THE LIBRARY) ... we can take our drinks in I presume?
ANN	Of course – and Larry, we have decided to do the Virginia Woolf book first and my one later.
LARRY	What?!
ANN	(APOLOGETICALLY) Well, Jennifer feels ...
JENNIFER	Yes, seems obvious to do the deeper one first – give Ms Woolf her rightful attention.
ROBERT	I'm all for that.
LARRY	(TO ANN) You mean we're doing that one now? First?
ROBERT	And Larry knows his stuff on Woolf, Jennifer.
JENNIFER	Fantastic.
ANN	This way everybody.
LARRY	(ANXIOUSLY TO ANN) Wait a minute!
ANN	(LOUDLY) Larry, do you want to nip upstairs to freshen up?
JENNIFER	(STOPS) Oh for heaven's sake – anyone for loos or whatever, please, now and not in the middle of our session.
ANN	Just Larry, I think, Jennifer.
JENNIFER	Very good but not too long, Larry. And everybody, mobiles off please. Really looking forward to this now. (GOES IN)
ROBERT	Mobile off. So let's go talk literature. (GOES IN)

DOROTHY	My glasses? Yes, here they are. (GOES IN)
LARRY	(QUIETLY) For Christ sake, Ann!
ANN	What was I to do? She made the decision!
LARRY	But what am I supposed to say in there? I know shag-all about that book.
ANN	But Robert said ...
LARRY	One sheet of paper – I can't keep repeating that like a shaggin' parrot!
ANN	Then that's why you should run up to Vincent now and get the rest.
LARRY	Jesus Christ, it's a nightmare – and the mask has dropped, Ann: that bastard is now threatening to drag us through the courts to get ...
JENNIFER	(OFF) Ann? Larry? We must begin please.
ANN	(CALLS) Coming, Jennifer. (TO LARRY) Will you just run up to Vincent and tell him to Google up ... (STOPS) What's that?
	ANN HAS SEEN THREE SHEETS OF THE GREEN A4 PAPER BEING SLID IN UNDER THE ENTRANCE DOOR.
LARRY	(GOES TO THE PAGES) Vincent!
ANN	Don't let him in or they'll all want to talk to him.
LARRY	(LOOKING AT THE PAGES) Three more pages about Virginia Woolf. (WHISPERS TO THE DOOR) Thanks, Vincent.
JENNIFER	(OFF) Ann, really, we must begin at once.
ANN	(CALLS) Coming, Jennifer. (TO LARRY) Will you come on!
LARRY	But I have to read them first.
ANN	No! Just bring them in – say you thought it all

up, wrote it all down and printed them all off yourself.

LARRY   (LOOKING AT THE PAGES) But what do they shaggin' mean?

ANN   (ANGRILY) It doesn't matter – just read them out. Now come on, they're all waiting. (GOING IN. BRIGHTLY) Sorry about that everyone. All set to start now, Jennifer.

LARRY   Jesus Christ help me! (GOING IN. TRYING HARD) Apologies everyone for that slight delay.

JENNIFER   (OFF) That's all right, Larry – you can sit over here beside Robert.

LARRY LOOKS TO HEAVEN AT THIS PROSPECT, GOES IN AND THE LIBRARY DOOR IS CLOSED.

END OF SCENE 1, ACT 1

Act 1, Scene 2

Forty-five minutes later. Room as before. Television black. Then the library door is angrily opened and Jennifer, Robert, Dorothy, Ann and Larry emerge. The meeting clearly has not gone well. Larry, alone, seems calm and confident.

JENNIFER   (ANGRILY TO ROBERT) I am *not* still carrying it on!

ROBERT   (ANGRILY) Well, you certainly haven't stopped!

JENNIFER   And you haven't stopped being an unelected Mr Chairman, Mr Know-All, Mr Alpha Dog, barking your opinions into everyone's face as if …

ROBERT   Someone had to take control!

JENNIFER   Which, in all our Book Clubs, no one ever had to do before.

ROBERT   No, because no one ever had the balls to confront you!

JENNIFER   Oh and that's why you came, is it? Well now we all know! Thank you!

PAUSE

DOROTHY   (QUIETLY) I think it was all my fault for …

JENNIFER   No, I understood your point perfectly, Dorothy – I just needed time to fully respond to it.

ANN   I think it was my fault for interrupting when Dorothy was saying that …

DOROTHY	No, you didn't interrupt, Ann.
ROBERT	No, you didn't, Ann.
LARRY	(WITH GREAT CONFIDENCE) Then I can only think that it must have been my fault for ...
DOROTHY	No, Larry ...
LARRY	(CONFIDENTLY) ... Yes, Dorothy, when I made my point to Jennifer ... (TAKES HIS GREEN PAGES FROM HIS POCKET) ... when I said from my notes that although (READS) 'Virginia Woolf may be rightly regarded as one of the foremost modernist literary figures of the twentieth century, is it not also a point that perhaps, by her death ...
JENNIFER	(QUIETLY) Jesus Christ!
LARRY	... that she seductively secured a false reputation and recognition, in the same way that her fellow feminist writer, Sylvia Path (SIC) in her similar suicide also ...'
JENNIFER	(EXPLODES) Plath, Plath, for God's sake, Plath!
LARRY	What?
JENNIFER	Do you even know who Sylvia Plath is?
ROBERT	Jennifer!
LARRY	Course I know who she is!
JENNIFER	(LOUDLY) Or will she soon become someone else again, just as Virginia Woolf can suddenly morph into Veronica Woolf or Vanessa Woolf or Victoria Woolf or whatever else you've learned from Wikipedia!
LARRY	What?
ROBERT	(HARD) Jennifer, will you for God's sake, once and for all, calm down!
	SILENCE

ANN	Just like to say that there are cheese and crackers here.
LARRY	(QUIETLY) Crackers is right!
DOROTHY	Thank you very much, Ann.
ROBERT	Yes, much obliged, Ann.
	PAUSE. ALL WILL EAT OR DRINK.
JENNIFER	(CONTROLLED) I said it before and I'll say it again, but I never approved the unwanted and unnecessary change to the basic and established dynamic of our Book Club – and clearly, I was right.
ROBERT	(LIGHTLY) You mean letting 'the men' in?
JENNIFER	Yes I do! In all our past debates, discussions or differences, we have never, ever, had a spectacle like we have just witnessed in there. Never.
DOROTHY	(QUIETLY) Well, there was the one occasion at Monica's …
JENNIFER	Which was different, Dorothy – there was too much drink taken at Monica's including, as I remember, not just wine but gin, vodka, whiskey, brandy and God knows what else.
DOROTHY	Yes.
JENNIFER	And it is so disappointing, when one has prepared so diligently for a meeting that it is allowed to descend into a dog-fight with an incorrigible alpha dog leading the pack.
	PAUSE
ANN	I'm really so sorry …
DOROTHY	For what, Ann?
ANN	Well, it's the first Book Club I've hosted and …

JENNIFER	Nobody is pointing the finger at you, Ann.
ROBERT	I don't think anyone is in any doubt where that finger is being pointed.
JENNIFER	Good.
ROBERT	And we're not a class of dull sixth-year students, afraid to challenge a point of view.
JENNIFER	Dull, sixth-year students have more maturity than you displayed in there!
ROBERT	(ANGRILY) And I suggest that if someone can't stand that kind of heat, they should stay out of the kitchen.
JENNIFER	Excuse me – I'm not in any kitchen.
ROBERT	Oh Jesus, when were you ever?
JENNIFER	(QUIETLY FURIOUS) Meaning exactly what?
ROBERT	Meaning exactly that you know exactly what I mean!
	PAUSE
DOROTHY	(QUIETLY) I wonder would it help if I very briefly finished my point and allowed everyone to respond and so conclude the issue and continue with the meeting?
ANN	(UNSURE) I think that might be a good idea …?
JENNIFER	It is (TOWARDS LARRY) provided no one is allowed to recite the same points ad infinitum (TOWARDS ROBERT) and no one vetoes intelligent reaction from those of us who really do have something to say!
DOROTHY	That sounds reasonable.
ANN	I think so too.
ROBERT	Larry?

LARRY   (GRUMPILY) I've no intention of ever opening my mouth again.

ROBERT   Ok. Then go ahead, Dorothy.

DOROTHY   (GENTLY) Well, my point was that I relate to Virginia Woolf as much through her life journey as through her magnificent, expressive and iconoclastic fiction.

ROBERT   Very nicely put, Dorothy.

DOROTHY   In her life, she had disruption and change with all its attendant anxieties imposed upon her and, for me personally, the resultant relationship she had with her husband Leonard, with Vita Sackville-West and Edith Sitwell are not unlike the great traumatic changes that I had imposed upon me when I, well, inherited my husband's estate – a millstone hung around my neck – which, through his secrecy and deception, I did not know existed.

ROBERT   As we are professionally and confidentially aware.

DOROTHY   In that moment, I felt that my life changed as Virginia's did – I was suddenly empowered, sought after, admired, celebrated, not for myself but for a position that was thrust upon me, as Virginia was with her literary gift, and suddenly she did not know who was friend, who was foe, who was vulture and who was dove – or what velvet glove held the iron fist. And it crushed her as it crushes me – because I have discovered, as she discovered that, in having more, I possess less – like her, not knowing who is false, who is true, who will betray me and who, in time of need, will stand faithfully by my side. And that, simply put, was my main point in my appreciation of her masterpiece *To the Lighthouse*.

PAUSE.

ANN   (GENTLY) And then so many of your dearest friends have died, Dorothy.

DOROTHY   Oh yes. And then comes the dark emptiness and the need to fill it. I know it well and wish I could stem its flood, as Virginia tried, through her exquisite fiction.

ROBERT   Excellent. Thank you, Dorothy. And any reactions? Jennifer?

JENNIFER   (COLDLY) Yes, I have two. The first is to thank Dorothy for that amazingly honest insight – and the second is to enquire why you are *still* behaving as though you are the chairman of our Book Club?

ROBERT   Thank you, Jennifer. Ann? Your reaction?

ANN   I just think it's all very sad.

ROBERT   Indeed. Thank you, Ann. Larry?

LARRY   (STILL ANNOYED) Me? I'm not supposed to know anything.

ROBERT   Thank you, Larry. So there we are, the discussion complete, everyone had their say and we are now clear to move on to our second book.

JENNIFER   Excuse me – have you no reaction of your own to Dorothy's contribution?

ROBERT   Of course – but Dorothy knows my reaction and she is very aware that when she needs a true friend, a confidant, a caring listener, she need look no further than my bank. And I am glad that you do, Dorothy.

DOROTHY   Thank you, Robert.

JENNIFER	So you have no literary reaction?
ROBERT	I gave it in there, and I think it was both well judged and appropriate. And now, with that, I think we can put Virginia Woolf to bed, so to speak, and I suggest we take a twenty-minute break to relax and chat amongst ourselves and partake of more of Ann's excellent food.
ANN	It's just cheese and ...
ROBERT	It is delicious, Ann, and we thank you – and then, in twenty minutes, all back to the library for our second book, which, tonight, is Harper Lee's *To Kill a Mockingbird*.
JENNIFER	Oh thank you!
ROBERT	No problem – and I, personally, will now take time out for a well-earned cheroot (TAKING THEM FROM HIS POCKET) ... and, I think, treat myself to one of these. (GOES TO THE WHISKEY)
JENNIFER	Excuse me – are you driving?
ROBERT	Not at the moment. I am standing.
JENNIFER	(ANGRILY) Impossible, juvenile, immature behaviour – however at our Book Clubs we do not permit smoking.
ROBERT	Out in your conservatory ok, Ann? Ok if I have my immature smoke and drink out there?
ANN	Oh of course. When he built it, Larry put in four Xpelair fans, especially for smokers, didn't you, Larry?
LARRY	(GRUMPILY) Yeah.
ANN	And I can also turn on our illuminated water features and fountains across our lawn, if you'd like to see them while you're out there.
ROBERT	That'd be great, Ann.

JENNIFER	And if you get bored, you can jump into one of the fountains.
ROBERT	(LIGHTLY) I may not do that, darling, but thanks for the suggestion. Twenty minutes, everybody.
	ROBERT GOES INTO THE CONSERVATORY, WITH HIS WHISKEY, CLOSING THE GLASS DOORS.
JENNIFER	(ANGRILY) This is so infuriating – and so typical of that man.
ANN	It's all right, Jennifer – I can turn the fans on now. (AT THE SWITCH)
JENNIFER	I mean his behaviour – that challenging, competitive, controlling attitude. Always the same!
ANN	(TURNS ON ANOTHER SWITCH) And this will show him the colour-changing fountain lights.
	THROUGH THE CONSERVATORY, WE CAN SEE THE GLOW OF THE CHANGING LIGHTS.
ROBERT	(SHOUTS FROM OFF) Oh lovely, Ann. Really lovely.
JENNIFER	And that does him no favours, Ann – pandering to him like that.
ANN	Ah I don't mind. Now, anyone for more wine, cheese, crackers? Larry, would you like something? You're very quiet.
LARRY	(ANNOYED. SUDDENLY GOES TOWARDS THE ENTRANCE DOOR) Back down in a minute.
ANN	Are you all right?
LARRY	Yes. The toilet.
ANN	You can use the downstairs one or …
LARRY	(LOUDLY) I don't think I need to be told what toilet to use in my own house!
	LARRY GOES ANGRILY, SLAMMING THE DOOR.

JENNIFER	That's my fault, Ann.
ANN	No no …
JENNIFER	No, what I said about Sylvia Plath – but that's all that man's fault (ROBERT) – he turns me into this defensive, aggressive creature, and I hate it and it's not going to continue. (POURING WINE) You don't mind?
ANN	No no, as much as you like.
JENNIFER	And perhaps you'll excuse me for five minutes but I really must talk to him, one to one, without an audience, when he's not being 'the big fellow', because this must end and it will. Back in five minutes, ladies – then, hopefully, we will have our traditional discussion for our second book. (GOING TOWARDS CONSERVATORY)
ANN	If it's cold out there …
JENNIFER	It will be fine. Five minutes. (GOES INTO CONSERVATORY)
	ANN AND DOROTHY TOGETHER. MORE RELAXED.
ANN	Oh God, this is dreadful. (HURRIEDLY POURS HERSELF A FULL GLASS OF WINE)
DOROTHY	It's not – it was an excellent debate …
ANN	And Larry galloping off, Robert running out, now Jennifer gone? I've never seen her so furious in my life. (DRINKS) Sorry, Dorothy, can I get you more water?
DOROTHY	No no, I'm perfectly all right.
ANN	And I should have had more food – maybe I'll do some sausage rolls and coffee …
DOROTHY	(HUNGRILY) Oh that would be excellent.

ANN   … after our next book.

DOROTHY   (DISAPPOINTED) Oh. Very good. (REACHES
           FOR A CRACKER)

JENNIFER   (OFF. LOUD AND SHRILL) No no no – it's what
           you always do and I'm sick and tired of it!

ANN   Oh God. (DRINKS) And that's my fault too: it
           was my suggestion that we should have men
           over.

DOROTHY   No, we all agreed.

ANN   But I started it …

JENNIFER   (OFF) Just shut up and listen!

ANN   God! (DRINKS)

DOROTHY   (CALMLY) Ann, a thought. You may not want to
           consider this, but do you think, from Jennifer's
           behaviour, that she perhaps knows something?

ANN   Knows something? Knows something about
           what?

DOROTHY   (CAREFULLY) About you and Robert?

ANN   Me and Robert? What about me and Robert?
           Whoever said anything about me and Robert?

DOROTHY   Well you did.

ANN   I did? When?

DOROTHY   In my car that night coming back from
           Monica's Book Club.

ANN   (ANNOYED) Jesus Christ, not again! If I hear
           one more thing that I'm supposed to have said
           in your car coming back from Monica's Book
           Club …

DOROTHY   I'm so sorry to mention it …

ANN   Dorothy, there is nothing to be sorry about
           because I have no recollection of ever saying

anything in your car, or anywhere else, about me and Robert or me and anyone and it is well known that when I get a bit tipsy that I say things that make no sense or ...

DOROTHY No, it was just when we were exchanging our little confidences and you said that you and Robert ...

ANN (ANGRILY) First Vincent and the budgie and now me and Robert! (PUTS HER GLASS DOWN) Well that's it: I'm never drinking another drop of anything, anywhere, ever again.

DOROTHY I only remember what you told me because Jennifer is so angry and I wondered ...

ANN Well Dorothy, there is no need to wonder because, if I told you what happened, then it happened and it was really nothing, it was just that, one evening, Robert and I happened to ... to ... to ... to ... (PANIC) ... Oh Jesus Christ, and then there's the diary that, like an eejit, I wrote it all down in and then I went and lost the feckin' thing! – and I can't find it anywhere, and I've searched high and low for that diary, and God only knows when someone – like Larry! – will suddenly find it and confront me with it – it's a twenty-four-hour-a-day nightmare – but I suppose I told you all about that too?

DOROTHY Well no, actually, you didn't tell me anything about that.

ANN I didn't? (BACKING DOWN) Well, that was because it was nothing – it was just ... (FIRMLY) Dorothy, if I didn't tell you about the diary, what exactly *did* I tell you?

DOROTHY Oh you just said that Larry needed some

	short-term bank loans for his business ... and you said you decided to make overtures to Robert ...
ANN	Overtures? What kind of overtures?
DOROTHY	Well, I cannot remember exactly ...
ANN	(RELIEVED) Right! – and that's because it was nothing to remember – it was just a meeting we had, and it only happened once, and it was ages ago, and anyway, in my diary, I wrote it all down in code, well not code, but kinda bad spelling ... (NEW DESPAIR) ... and Jesus Christ how I've searched for that diary – there's nowhere I haven't looked for it – I even wondered had I thrown it into the green bin by mistake, then I thought maybe when Aisling was packing for Australia did she throw it into her luggage by mistake, or did I hide it somewhere really secret in the house that I can't remember – and if Larry ever finds it! – Jesus, is it any wonder I drink too much, but one thing for sure, I'm off it now, forever, finished with the stuff, for good!
DOROTHY	I'm sorry, Ann – I was just wondering why Jennifer was so angry at Robert ...
ANN	Well, it has nothing to do with me!
DOROTHY	No, of course not – and she has been very friendly towards you.
ANN	And why wouldn't she be? I did nothing. (LOOKING TOWARDS THE CONSERVATORY. SUDDEN PANIC) Oh Jesus Christ, here she is now! She's coming!
DOROTHY	Don't worry – I'm sure she suspects nothing.
ANN	I know she doesn't – because there is nothing to suspect!

JENNIFER COMES FROM THE CONSERVATORY.
SHE STANDS STERNLY IN THOUGHT.

ANN (NERVOUSLY) Welcome back, Jennifer – everything all right?

JENNIFER (BRIGHTLY) I think so and good news, fingers crossed, it may be peace in our time.

DOROTHY Oh excellent.

JENNIFER I think, after some explanations, Robert now understands the workings of our club.

DOROTHY Oh that's good.

JENNIFER To be honest, he is really a good fellow, works really hard, is a great father, the kids adore him, but put him into any competitive situation and he has to take control, overpower and win!

DOROTHY My late husband, Godfrey, had to stop playing golf for the same reason.

JENNIFER Oh Robert abandoned squash completely before he killed someone – took up martial arts instead. By the way, Ann, I love your water features and your conservatory is just beautiful.

ANN Oh, thank you, Jennifer, I'm delighted. Some more wine?

JENNIFER Why not. Then I really think we should make our way back.

ANN Dorothy?

DOROTHY I still have my water.

JENNIFER (WATCHING. TO ANN) You're also on water?

ANN Yes, I think so.

JENNIFER (LIGHTLY) Oh shame. I think we all like you best when you're slightly tipsy.

LAUGHTER FROM JENNIFER AND DOROTHY,

AND FEIGNED LAUGHTER FROM ANN AS LARRY
COMES IN.

JENNIFER   Ah Larry – we are just about to resume.

ANN   And Jennifer was admiring our conservatory
           and our illuminations – (TO JENNIFER) all
           designed and built by Larry.

JENNIFER   Oh well done, Larry – excellent.

LARRY   (ANNOYED) Thanks – and I just want to
           correct something that was said earlier about
           me – a reference to …

ANN   Now, Larry, that's all …

LARRY   … a reference to what I know or do not know
           about Sylvia Plath.

JENNIFER   Yes, Larry, and that was my fault for …

LARRY   … and, at the time, I wasn't afforded the time
           or the opportunity to contradict this …

ANN   Larry …

LARRY   … and I want to say now that I *do* know who
           Sylvia Plath is …

JENNIFER   (CONTRITE) … of course, and …

LARRY   (ALMOST A MEMORISED PERFORMANCE)
           She was married to Ted Hughes who was the
           poet laureate, and her poems are world famous,
           poems like 'Blackberring' and 'Crossing the
           River' and … and … (STOPS) … and another
           one … and her poems deal with confessional
           poetry about details of her own life and she
           committed suicide by putting her head in the
           oven, just as Virginia Woolf also did, except she
           done it by walking into a river and that was the
           point I was making that they both had that in
           common, apart from their writings and that's
           what makes us always think of them together.

LARRY FINISHES, ALMOST EXHAUSTED, HEAVES A SIGH OF RELIEF.

JENNIFER   Well that is excellent, Larry – you certainly know your Plath and your Woolf.

DOROTHY   Some excellent points.

JENNIFER   Absolutely.

ANN   Very good, Larry.

LARRY   And all the notes I had on Virginia Woolf at that meeting were my own too, ones that I wrote out and run off.

ROBERT COMES IN FROM THE CONSERVATORY.

ROBERT   Ah here we are all again.

JENNIFER   Yes darling, all set to resume … and if anyone wants the loo or anything, do so now please.

ROBERT   No, I'm fine.

DOROTHY   And Larry has been detailing his comparisons between Sylvia Plath and Virginia Woolf …

JENNIFER   (LIGHTLY) That he was prevented from doing earlier for some reason! *Mea culpa*, Larry.

ROBERT   (LIGHTLY) *Mea maxima culpa* – apologies, Larry.

LARRY   It's all right – I said it all now anyway.

JENNIFER   Excellent. And now, Ann, we should go in?

ANN   Oh please. Bring your drinks – and crackers, Dorothy, if you wish.

DOROTHY   Just one or two perhaps.

ROBERT   I loved this book, Larry.

LARRY   Me too – and I'll be in later.

ANN   No Larry, we're starting now!

LARRY   You can all start, I'll be in later.

DOROTHY   Or we can wait?

LARRY	No no, I'll be in later.
JENNIFER	You're sure, Larry?
LARRY	Yes, I'll be in later.
JENNIFER	Very well. Everyone else, in now, please. (GOING IN WITH DOROTHY AND ROBERT. NOW URGENTLY) And as soon as you're ready, Ann, Larry. (GOES IN, CLOSES THE DOOR)
ANN	(ANNOYED) What's this about? Why are you waiting till later to come in?
LARRY	(ANGRILY) If you must know, I have no shaggin' intention of going in at all – I'm sick to my stomach of being made a laughing stock by that stuck-up bitch …
ANN	She's not!
LARRY	Did you not hear all the crap I had to learn off from Vincent?
ANN	Yes, and all that was forgotten until you dragged it all up again!
LARRY	It wasn't forgotten and then I had to recite it for her as if I was back in school …
ANN	No one asked you to …
LARRY	… and I'm not sitting in there again, afraid to open my mouth …
ANN	But you know all about this book.
LARRY	There's always things I don't know that everyone else knows – and that smug husband of hers is all on to drag us through the courts, and, mark my words, we'll end up selling this house and everything in it.
ANN	Oh don't start that again!
LARRY	I'm not starting it – he is!
	LIBRARY DOOR OPENS.

JENNIFER	(LOOKS OUT. URGENTLY) Ann? Are you ready?
ANN	Coming, Jennifer.
JENNIFER	Soon as you can. (GOES IN, CLOSING THE DOOR)
ANN	(ANGRILY TO LARRY) So are you coming or not?
LARRY	Are you deaf? No, I'm not!
ANN	Right, stay then – but don't blame me when all you're saying happens – just remember I did my best to get you on his good side – but if you want to spend the rest of your life ducking and diving and running and hiding …
LARRY	I'll be here when you come out.
ANN	Oh thanks very much – and if it's not too much trouble, while you are out here, still hiding, would you mind turning off the fans and the garden lights and make sure that jailbird brother of yours doesn't walk in here – or is that asking too much of you? (GOING INTO THE LIBRARY. VERY SWEETLY) So sorry, everybody – Larry is still detained but I think we can begin.
	THE LIBRARY DOOR IS CLOSED.
LARRY	(TO HIMSELF) Detained! Being made to stand up in front of them like a bleedin' dunce, in my own house, and answering questions about poems and Sylvia shaggin' Plath.
	LARRY HAS GONE TO THE SWITCHES AND TURNS OFF THE FANS AND THE CONSERVATORY/GARDEN LIGHTS. HE COMES BACK INTO THE ROOM. SUDDENLY, THE HOUSE PHONE RINGS.
LARRY	Oh Jesus! I hope this isn't Aisling. (PICKS IT

UP) Hello? Oh hello, Aisling. (LISTENS) You want to do it now? The webcam and all the …? (LISTENS) No, she's not here but I think I know how to … (LISTENS) Yes yes, of course I do … yes, right away. Ok love, ok, see you there. (PUTS THE PHONE DOWN) Jesus Christ! (GOES QUICKLY TO THE COMPUTER. LOST) Why couldn't she have written all that stuff down? What was it? Snooze and mouse … mouse … (MOVES THE MOUSE. THE SITE APPEARS ON THE PLASMA SCREEN) Oh thank God! And her name is there … and 'accept' there … and …

LARRY HITS A KEY AND AISLING APPEARS ON THE SCREEN. SHE IS DRESSED FOR GOING OUT.

LARRY   Ah there you are, love – can you see me?

AISLING   Yes, Dad, perfectly – well done! Where's Mum?

LARRY   She's in at the Book Club, love – I'm going in soon.

AISLING   Oh ok. And where's Uncle Vincent?

LARRY   Vincent? He's up in his room. Is anything wrong, love?

AISLING   No Dad, just that there was something I wanted to say earlier to Mum, and I tried to get back but there was no one there …

LARRY   And what was it you wanted to say?

AISLING   Well, it'd be better if I told Mum.

LARRY   I can get her for you if it's urgent …

AISLING   No, it's all right. Is Robert Travers from the bank there?

LARRY   Robert? Yes and his wife Jennifer and Dorothy, all in at the Book Club.

AISLING	OK that's cool – so just listen now, Dad, and don't get annoyed – it's just something that's been bothering me a bit – you know how Uncle Vincent has this quick temper …
LARRY	No, he hasn't …
AISLING	(ANNOYED) Dad! What about the budgie he crushed to death in his fist? And you know very well what he was in jail for in England, how he tried to crucify that man to the floor …
LARRY	For God's sake, Aisling, he never crucified anyone …
AISLING	Just listen, Dad!
LARRY	… and all that happened years ago and you know we never talk about it anymore …
AISLING	Dad, we know what he did and I was thinking he might do the same again if he finds out, or hears about, anything that happened down at the bank …
LARRY	The bank?
AISLING	The bank when I was temping there with Sarah Murray, Dad.
LARRY	This is Robert Travers' bank?
AISLING	Yes and the thing is that, after we left, Sarah started going around Dublin telling everyone what happened to her – not to me, Dad, to *her*! – in his private office.
LARRY	Whose private office?
AISLING	Mr Travers' private office!
LARRY	Jesus Christ, are you telling me that that bastard tried to …?
AISLING	Not to me, Dad, never to me.

LARRY	Not to you but you're still telling me that in his private office …?
AISLING	Only to Sarah, Dad, and maybe not to her because Sarah is a terrible spoofer, she makes things up …
LARRY	But why would she make up something like that?
AISLING	Dad, she just does! But listen because I have to go soon – what's bothering me now is that Vincent is in the same house as Robert Travers and if he heard any of these rumours about me or Sarah …
LARRY	About you?!
AISLING	No, about Sarah, just Sarah! Because lots of people heard them and it was because of similar rumours that Uncle Vincent crucified that man to the floor in England …
LARRY	Aisling, he crucified nobody!
AISLING	All right – threatened to!
LARRY	(FURIOUSLY) And Aisling, I want to know now exactly what that bastard did or didn't do to you or to Sarah when …
AISLING	Now this is why I wanted to tell Mum, not you!
LARRY	Well now you're telling me and I want to know exactly what happened …
AISLING	To me, nothing! To Sarah, probably nothing – but I don't want to be out here and Uncle Vincent there with his quick temper because if he half heard something down at the newsagent or …
LARRY	I'm getting your mother …
AISLING	No Dad, I have to go. All I want you to do

is, if it comes up, to make sure that Uncle Vincent knows that nothing happened to me – (ANGRILY) the last thing I want to hear out here is someone else finishing up like my budgie or like that man nailed to the floor! All right, Dad?

LARRY   No, it's not all right – hold on there until …

AISLING   I really got to go, Dad. Thanks. Love you.

AISLING IS GONE FROM THE SCREEN, REPLACED BY THE WEBCAM SITE. LARRY FRANTICALLY HITS THE KEYBOARD TO GET HER BACK. THE SCREEN WILL SOON GO TO BLACK. ALL AS:

LARRY   Aisling? Aisling? Jesus Christ Almighty, I'm getting to the bottom of this, Book Club or no Book Club.

LARRY GOES TO THE LIBRARY DOOR. KNOCKS AND OPENS IT.

LARRY   (VERY POLITELY) Excuse me a minute …

JENNIFER   (OFF) Oh come in, Larry, come in.

LARRY   No – Ann, can you come out please?

ANN   (OFF) What, now? We're in the middle of …

LARRY   (ANGRILY) Yes, now, please! Now! Thank you!

ANN COMES OUT, CLOSING THE DOOR.

ANN   (ANGRILY) What is it, for God's sake? Just as everything is going great again …

LARRY   (ANGRILY) Aisling was back on that web thing …

ANN   When, now?

LARRY   Yes now! – and she told me something that nearly has me wanting to throw up, here, in this very room!

ANN   Oh God, what's happened to her?

LARRY	It's not to her – it's what'll happen to that bastard in there, that bloody sex maniac, if only half of what I just heard about him is true.
ANN	(FEARFULLY SUSPECTING) Who, Robert?
LARRY	(FURIOUS) Yes, Robert! Mr Success, Mr Big-Time Operator, the great know-all, and now I'm hearing what he gets up to in his spare time, with *my* family …
ANN	(REALISING) Oh God.
LARRY	… and if there's only that much truth in what Aisling has told me, I swear to Christ I'll go out and get a lump hammer and I'll smash his shaggin' skull open so he'll never go near anyone again, in or out of this family, this household, Ann!
ANN	(PANIC) Oh Jesus Christ – she's the one that has it!
LARRY	I don't know what she has or doesn't have – but I've a good mind to walk in there now and kick the truth out of him and then …
ANN	No Larry, don't, just calm down and I'll explain something to you because, no matter what you heard, it's nothing, it really is nothing, Larry, I swear it.
LARRY	Yes and that's how Aisling tried to shut me up too, saying it was nothing!
ANN	And she's right, it is nothing – and I'll tell you now all about Robert.
LARRY	Good! Because I'm sick and tired of being the last to know anything in this house …
ANN	You're not the last because I'm going to tell you now … (SUDDENLY ANGRY) … and is Aisling

	out of her mind or on drugs or something to be telling you this!
LARRY	She wanted to only tell you!
ANN	Of course she did – (CONTROLLED) and now, listen, stay calm because all that happened was that I knew you wanted that loan and I knew Robert would turn you down …
LARRY	(ANGRILY) What has the loan got to do with …?
ANN	Just listen! (CAREFULLY) One day – by coincidence when you were down in Wexford – Robert dropped over here, just for a chat about the loan and everything, and we had a drink or two, to be social, and what happened then, no matter what Aisling says is in the diary, was nothing, Larry, nothing – and I should never have wrote it and I know that maybe she's afraid with Robert here now, but I swear to God, all the stuff I wrote was for fun, it's all makey-up, like writing a book, Larry – you know how I always wanted to write something, stories or a book, like Virginia Woolf – so there was never anything that really happened, like in the bedroom … or on the stairs … or in the wardrobe or whatever she said is in the diary, that was all makey-up, like me trying to be a writer and you got the loan on merit, Larry, merit! and it had nothing to do with anything else, nothing, I swear it, and that's the truth.
	PAUSE.
LARRY	Jesus Christ, Ann, what are you telling me?
ANN	The truth, Larry – nothing happened between me and Robert, nothing ever, down here or anywhere.

LARRY	But Aisling wasn't talking about you.
ANN	What?
LARRY	She was talking about Robert and Sarah.
ANN	Sarah? Who … who's Sarah?
LARRY	Her friend, young Sarah Murray – but now you're telling me …
ANN	What?! No, no, I'm not, I'm not telling you anything …
LARRY	Jesus Christ!
ANN	No, Larry, listen, just calm down and let me explain what I was really saying …
LARRY	Jesus Christ Almighty!
ANN	Just listen – I can explain it all and it's really very simple …
	A KNOCK ON THE ENTRANCE DOOR. IT OPENS. A QUIET, GAUNT MAN IN HIS MID-FIFTIES STANDS IN. HE WEARS GLASSES. THIS IS VINCENT. ANN SEES HIM FIRST.
ANN	Oh for God's sake – Vincent! What do you want?
LARRY	(SHOUTS) Vincent, get out! Get back upstairs before they all see you!
	THE LIBRARY DOOR OPENS. JENNIFER APPEARS.
JENNIFER	Ann, we cannot continue if … (SEES VINCENT) Oh hello, are you one of the husbands arriving for our Book Club?
ANN	(AWKWARDLY) No no, Jennifer, this is actually …
LARRY	(LOUDLY AND ANGRILY) Yes, on top of everything else, as if I hadn't heard enough already, as if things were not bad enough, this is my brother, this is Vincent!

JENNIFER (IN AWE) Oh my God – how lovely to meet you.

BLACKOUT.

END OF ACT 1

Act 2, Scene 1

Thirty minutes later. The room is the same, just a little more tidy. On the table, some plates of finger food, fresh glasses and a cut drizzle cake. Library door open. Only Larry in the room. He is at the computer, with the instruction book in one hand, angrily trying to get online. The TV screen shows the webcam site and will soon go to snooze.

LARRY   Goddamn, bloody, blasted, useless heap of crappy instructions! (THROWS THE BOOK ASIDE)

                 ANN COMES IN THROUGH THE ENTRANCE DOOR. SHE CARRIES A PLATE OF SAUSAGE ROLLS. SHE SEEMS ALMOST TOO UPBEAT AND POSITIVE, AS SHE CHECKS AND SETS THE FOOD OUT.

ANN   (TO HERSELF) Now. Sausage rolls at last. And fresh glasses here. And I think they liked the cheese, so they'll like these cheese-and-grape sticks. Very nice. And a nice drizzle cake, neatly sliced. Yes, they'll be peckish after seeing all of Vincent's projects up there. But we mustn't forget this is our Book Club and we still have our second book to do. Jennifer won't allow us to forget that anyway. (BRIGHTLY TO LARRY) What were you doing there, Larry? Don't lose Aisling's site, in case she wants to reach us again.

LARRY   (ANGRILY) I'm trying to find a way to reach *her* again!

ANN	(BRIGHTLY) Oh? Why?
LARRY	Why? I'll tell you why! Because, whether you like it or not, I'm going to get to the bottom of this.
ANN	(MORE ANNOYED) The bottom of what, exactly?
LARRY	You know bloody-well what – first, Aisling and has she been molested by that bastard up there …
ANN	But you said she distinctly told you she wasn't!
LARRY	There's never smoke without fire.
ANN	There is if nothing happened to her, which is what she said!
LARRY	And then there's you!
ANN	Me?
LARRY	Yes you, and that same pervert – first your admission and then your denial …
ANN	(CASUALLY) How many times do I have to say it? – there's nothing to admit or to deny – I was writing a book, making up a story, out of my head …
LARRY	Yes, about you and him!
ANN	Not about him.
LARRY	About who then?
ANN	About anyone.
LARRY	Called Robert.
ANN	Called anything.
LARRY	All in your diary?
ANN	That I use as a notebook, for notes about what I'm making up in my head …
LARRY	About carrying on in our bedroom and on our stairs and in our wardrobe!

ANN	Not 'our' anything – it's all out of my head.
LARRY	But how did it get *into* your head?
ANN	Because I make it up and because I make it up means I'm not doing it!
LARRY	Oh is that so?
ANN	Of course it's so – do you think that Agatha Christie was out murdering people before she started writing books about murder?
LARRY	Oh full of excuses but the fact remains that this is the first I ever heard of you being a writer or wanting to be one.
ANN	No it's not – I always talked about it …
LARRY	Not to me!
ANN	Yes to you, and I sang about it. What was my favourite song, my party piece for years – (SINGS) 'If they asked me I could write a book'.
LARRY	I never even knew you knew that.
ANN	Of course you did.
LARRY	I didn't, but I do know one thing – that under this roof we have a sex maniac, an adulterer and a shaggin' whoremaster!
ANN	Ah what are you talking about?
LARRY	Him! Under this roof!
ANN	He's done nothing!
LARRY	I'm not an eejit, Ann!
ANN	(SUDDENLY VERY ANGRY) Well, you're acting like one now – and, Larry Henderson, if you want to accuse anyone, accuse your own brother, also under this roof and a convicted jailbird for having caused the death of an innocent man because – like you! – he *thought* the poor devil was guilty of something.

LARRY	That 'poor devil' was guilty of molesting a young …
ANN	He was innocent!
LARRY	And anyway, Vincent only threatened him …
ANN	Yes, with six-inch nails and a knife! Him and his temper and his late vocation for the priesthood, seeing badness everywhere …
LARRY	(LOUDLY) All lies, Ann, lies!
ANN	(LOUDLY AND ANGRILY) No, the truth, Larry, but you never want the truth – not about Vincent, not about what Aisling says or I say, not about this recession, not about what it is doing to us, and not about the people we have to go out and meet and talk to and lick up to if we are to have any chance of getting through it!

THE DOOR OPENS AND DOROTHY POLITELY LOOKS IN.

DOROTHY	Sorry for interrupting …
ANN	(SUDDENLY POLITE) No no, come in, Dorothy, we were just discussing … the next book. Are you all finished with Vincent?
DOROTHY	Well not quite – but we were wondering if he may join us for our final session, if you are both agreeable?
ANN	What? Oh of course we are – aren't we, Larry?
LARRY	(AGHAST) Who? Vincent?
DOROTHY	He is most interesting and very informed and I think, we all think, could make excellent contributions.
ANN	Really? Oh well, of course, Dorothy.
DOROTHY	Oh good, I will tell them.

ANN	And then all come down when you're ready.
DOROTHY	We will. (GOING)
ANN	And tell them I have sausage rolls.
DOROTHY	(ENTHUSIASTIC) Oh yes, I will.
	DOROTHY GOES, CLOSING THE DOOR.
ANN	(CONTINUING ANGRILY TO LARRY) And I'm not going back over Vincent again, he did what he did, and now he's here with us and, as long as he doesn't stay forever, I'm willing to put up with that …
LARRY	He's only here until the priests decide where …
ANN	He could have gone back to them as soon as he was out of jail – but that's all right, with Aisling gone there's more room in the house …
LARRY	And I'm not to blame for Aisling going to Australia.
ANN	(ANGRILY) Well, let's not get into that! – we now have one more book to do, so let's get through that – and just remember that these are important people and they want to be our friends, and they have influence, and they are only here for two more hours, *maximum*!
LARRY	And you just remember I'm not an eejit.
ANN	(HARD) And here they are!
	A SOUND OUTSIDE. THE DOOR OPENS. JENNIFER AND ROBERT COME IN. ROBERT HOLDS THE REMAINS OF A GLASS OF WHISKEY. BOTH IN GOOD FORM.
JENNIFER	(AS SHE ENTERS) But where does he get so many of them?

ROBERT	(AS HE ENTERS) Everyone uses matches at some time ...
JENNIFER	Ann – this is truly our most exciting Book Club ever!
ANN	Oh do you think so really?
JENNIFER	Without a doubt. And Larry, your brother is just so amazing.
ROBERT	And talented.
JENNIFER	Oh so talented – are there any other builders in your family?
LARRY	What?
ROBERT	Because you're a builder, he's a builder ...
LARRY	(GRUMPILY) ... a builder in matchsticks ...
ROBERT	Yes, but still a builder.
JENNIFER	Absolutely. So do you have any brothers who are builders?
ROBERT	Or their sons who are builders?
LARRY	No, I haven't.
ROBERT	Your father then, he must have been a builder.
JENNIFER	Oh yes!
ROBERT	He surely was a builder – was he a builder, your father?
LARRY	He was a milkman.
JENNIFER	A milkman? Really? That's amazing.
ANN	(TRYING) But maybe, Larry, in his spare time, as a hobby, your father built things out of matchsticks?
LARRY	(ADAMANT) He didn't.
ROBERT	Or lollypop sticks?
JENNIFER	Yes, Vincent first built the Sydney Opera House out of lollypop sticks.

LARRY	He didn't build anything out of matchsticks or lollypop sticks or chopsticks or any other kind of sticks. He was a milkman.
ROBERT	(JOKING) Maybe out of milk-bottle tops then?
JENNIFER	(LAUGHING) Don't be silly, Robert.
ROBERT	Yes, sorry Larry, little joke – seriously, lovely work. Vincent. (DRINKS OFF HIS WHISKEY)
JENNIFER	(QUIETLY, OF THE WHISKEY) That's enough now.
ROBERT	They're only halves.
JENNIFER	It's your third.
ANN	(LOUDLY) And now, everybody, we have sausage rolls.
JENNIFER	Oh my goodness, Ann, is there no end to your *amuse-bouche*?
ANN	(LOST, BUT RECOVERING) Just help yourselves, everybody. And cheese sticks. And cake, big and small slices. But I suggest sausage rolls first, while they are hot.
ROBERT	Absolutely agree, Ann. (MERRILY TAKES ONE) Why did the sausage roll?
JENNIFER	(TAKING ONE. MERRILY) Don't start, Robert.
ROBERT	Larry? Because it saw the apple crumble.
ANN	Oh very good, Robert.
ROBERT	Why did the tomato blush?
JENNIFER	Don't encourage him.
ROBERT	Because it saw the salad dressing.
ANN	(BRIGHTLY) Oh very good.
LARRY	(MOVES AWAY) Jaysus!
ANN	(QUICKLY) And where is Dorothy?
ROBERT	I think she's up there counting the matchsticks

in St Peter's Basilica.

JENNIFER   She is absolutely enthralled by all Vincent has done, as are we – and Vincent says that he is going to bring down the Sagrada Família.

ROBERT   That's the church they've been building in Barcelona for 126 years.

JENNIFER   Yes, but Vincent is going to complete it from his own design. How brilliant is that? What a mind, despite what ... (STOPS)

ROBERT   Yes exactly – and on that subject, Larry, and we don't wish to pry ...

JENNIFER   No no, of course not – but we simply do not remember the case at all – well, not the details ...

ROBERT   We know it was in England and it was contended that Vincent was trying to frighten the other guy who was up to something ...?

ANN   (DEFLECTING) Well, it was all over four years ago ...

ROBERT   (EATING) Yes, but do I remember that he – Vincent – was going to crucify him to the floor?

LARRY   (ANGRILY) No, you don't remember that because that never happened.

ROBERT   No, because the police burst in ...

LARRY   No, because he never intended to do it in the first place.

ROBERT   Yes but wasn't there a hammer and nails when ...

LARRY   Yes because they belonged to the other fella who happened to be a carpenter.

ROBERT   A carpenter? Of course – hammer and nails.

ANN   Exactly – and honestly, you only have to look

	at Vincent to know that he could never …
JENNIFER	Well yes, exactly, you can see that he's as gentle as a lamb …
ANN	Exactly.
ROBERT	So it was really only a threat to crucify him and to castrate him?
ANN	No no, Robert!
LARRY	(ANGRILY) And that's exactly how wrong information gets out because that never happened. Never!
ROBERT	But wasn't he shouting that he'd castrate him when the neighbours phoned the police?
ANN	No, it was the wrong word, wasn't it, Larry?
LARRY	First, he wasn't shouting anything, he doesn't shout – what he was saying was that he was only going to castigate the man, give him a fright, teach him a lesson, that's what that word means, to castigate.
ROBERT	Of course.
LARRY	But the neighbours and the English police picked it up wrong …
ANN	And we think that's how it got into the papers …
ROBERT	And by then the charge was manslaughter …
LARRY	Except that it shouldn't have been manslaughter or anything because how was Vincent to know that the man had a heart condition and would suddenly drop dead – so it should have been case dismissed.
JENNIFER	(SUMMING UP, AS IN CLASS) Yes, but isn't this the most wonderful outcome to such a tragic set of circumstances – how Vincent, suddenly

taken from his quiet life and incarcerated, immediately channelled his energies and discovered his gifts and revealed an inner genius. When we consider that, let us think of the parallels in literature, and what comes to mind? Alexandre Dumas' *Count of Monte Cristo*, Solzhenitsyn's *Gulag Archipelago*, even Henri Charrière's *Papillon*. The list goes on.

JENNIFER HAS TURNED TO ANN FOR A CONTINUATION. ANN LOST. THEN:

ROBERT   (MERRILY) I can see us all having to write essays on this for next week!

JENNIFER   (MERRILY) Not necessarily.

ANN   (RELIEVED) That's very funny.

JENNIFER   But honestly, someone should write a book about it – if any of us had the talent to do that.

ANN   Yes. (QUICKLY) Another sausage roll anyone?

JENNIFER   (TAKES ONE) Why not.

ROBERT   (TAKES ONE) Delicious, Ann.

JENNIFER   But, everyone, we must not lose sight of our own Book Club proper – and we do have one more book to finish.

ROBERT   *To Kill a Mockingbird* – and I may have some interesting comments on a latter-day Boo Radley not a million miles away from us.

JENNIFER   All for later, Robert.

ROBERT   Absolutely.

THE DOOR OPENS. DOROTHY ENTERS. SHE CARRIES A SMALL CARDBOARD BOX.

DOROTHY   (LOOKING BACK) Careful now, Vincent, careful.

ANN   Which one have you got there, Vincent?

DOROTHY   It's Notre Dame cathedral in Paris.

JENNIFER   How fantastic.

ROBERT   Wonderful.

            VINCENT COMES IN CARRYING A MATCHSTICK-
            MADE MODEL OF NOTRE DAME.

JENNIFER   Vincent, that's magnificent – but not the
            Sagrada Família of Barcelona?

VINCENT   (QUIETLY) Dorothy expressed a preference for
            Notre Dame.

DOROTHY   I once visited Notre Dame with a very good
            friend, who was Parisian, and she knew every
            stone, every turret, every gargoyle in that cathe-
            dral and this is perfection, exact in every detail.

JENNIFER   Isn't it just.

DOROTHY   (OPENS THE CARDBOARD BOX) And these are
            the tools Vincent uses to build his churches
            and cathedrals – glue, cut-up matches,
            measuring tape, set square, knife for cutting
            and trimming, tiny paint brushes.

ANN   Put it down here, Vincent.

JENNIFER   It looks so majestic.

ROBERT   Dorothy, you should take a photo of it and
            send it to your Parisian friend.

DOROTHY   Oh I would love to do that …

ANN   We have a camera here somewhere … (GETS IT)

ROBERT   Oh you must do it, Dorothy – she'd love that.

JENNIFER   Oh yes, I'd say she'd be very impressed.

DOROTHY   Yes she would, but unfortunately she is dead.

            ANN'S CAMERA HAS ALREADY FLASHED. EVERY-
            ONE STOPS.

ROBERT   (TO DOROTHY) What?

DOROTHY	She was one of my closest friends, my confidante really, but last year, two weeks before I planned to visit her, she suddenly collapsed in the street and died.
ANN	Oh.
JENNIFER	(SYMPATHETICALLY TO DOROTHY) *Quelle dommage.*
DOROTHY	Thank you.
ANN	That's terrible, Dorothy. (OF THE PHOTO-GRAPH) I'll delete that.
DOROTHY	So this (THE MODEL) brings back such lovely memories, Vincent.
VINCENT	I am very pleased.
ANN	Yes. Now, sausage rolls here, Dorothy and Vincent – and water for you, Dorothy – and Vincent?
VINCENT	Water too, please.
ANN	And water for me. (POURING)
ROBERT	(MERRILY) Good God, it's the Book Club at the Oasis! Red for me, I think.
JENNIFER	Robert!
ROBERT	Just a glass. Thank you, Ann.
ANN	Jennifer, help yourself.
JENNIFER	Thank you, Ann. And may I ask Vincent, before we recommence our Book Club session – and you are most welcome to be part of it, Vincent …
VINCENT	Thank you.
JENNIFER	… but did you always want to build churches and cathedrals or monuments before you were suddenly … (STOPS) … before you began to build them or was this just something that

	came to you when you were ... (STOPS) ... well, when you had more time on your hands?
VINCENT	(GENTLY) Well, I always loved beauty and delicacy and the simplicity of innocent belief and I always admired the manifestation of such belief in beautiful buildings – be they cathedrals, mosques, temples, totem poles even ...
JENNIFER	... absolutely agree ...
VINCENT	... and I equally despised, abhorred and loathed anything that defiled, destroyed or abused such beauty, innocence or perfection and, not surprisingly perhaps, the first church I built was, if you know it, the bombed-out Kaiser Wilhelm Memorial Church in Berlin?
ROBERT	Oh yes, we have wonderful photos of that.
JENNIFER	We just loved that church and all it represents and we loved Berlin, adored Berlin.
ROBERT	Have you ever been to Berlin, Dorothy?
DOROTHY	Oh yes, I had a dear friend there who has since very tragically died.
ROBERT	Right. So, Vincent, you began with that church?
VINCENT	Yes, because I had seen photographs of it before its destruction, in all its beauty, its dignity and magnificence ...
ROBERT	I can imagine.
VINCENT	(SUDDENLY MORE PASSIONATE) ... and then I saw it as it is now: defiled, ravished and abused by the mindless barbarians who care little for beauty and only see their own transitory, selfish needs – (ON HIS FEET, ANGRILY) and I could have rebuilt it as it once was, I could have, but I decided: better

to leave it and show what we, any of us, all of us are capable of, when we slide to our most evil levels, afforded to us by power, privilege or position. That's what cannot be forgotten!

VINCENT HAS REACHED AN ANGRY CRESCEN-DO, HIS FIST HELD HIGH. HE NOW, REALISING, OPENS HIS FIST AND WE SEE THAT HE HOLDS HIS CRUSHED SAUSAGE ROLL IN A MANNER THAT REMINDS US OF HOW DOROTHY, EARLIER, HAD DESCRIBED HIM HOLDING THE CRUSHED BUDGIE. NOW, SUDDENLY CALM, HE PUTS THE CRUSHED SAUSAGE ROLL DOWN AND SITS. PAUSE. THEN:

JENNIFER   (GENTLY) But later, as time passed, you saw beauty again and you built more magnificent churches – and we have seen, upstairs, how you are planning to complete the beautiful Sagrada Família.

ANN   Oh Vincent always loved beautiful things. And you did too, Larry.

LARRY   (GRUMPILY) No. It was always him.

ROBERT   No Larry, look at this house and all the houses you built and refurbished …

DOROTHY   People still admire the conservatory you built for me after my husband died.

JENNIFER   You were the most sought-after, Larry – we always intended to get you …

ROBERT   Absolutely – and that cobble-locking pavement you put down outside Mooney's mini-market is a work of art.

JENNIFER   Oh yes, it certainly is.

LARRY   They're just jobs.

VINCENT   No Larry, growing up, you had a great sense of

	beauty.
LARRY	No I hadn't.
VINCENT	You had.
ANN	I'm sure you had, Larry.
VINCENT	(LIGHTLY) Who collected all those coloured stamps, the big Russian ones, and pasted them into those scrapbooks with flowers on the front?
LARRY	Ah for God's sake!
ANN	Did you, Larry?
JENNIFER	Ahhhhhhh.
VINCENT	The loveliest stamps you ever saw.
LARRY	Jaysus, we all did that.
VINCENT	Not all of us, but you did – and you painted your bicycle with all those colours and you were the snappiest dresser growing up …
ANN	You were! And your hair, falling into your eyes …
LARRY	Will you stop!
ANN	(MERRILY) Very good-looking you were.
JENNIFER	I can believe it.
VINCENT	And all the birds you had.
ROBERT	Did you?
ANN	What birds? Who were they?
VINCENT	The feathery ones.
ANN	Oh them.
ROBERT	Panic over, Larry!
LARRY	Mammy and Daddy had them, not me.
VINCENT	No, you too, Larry.
ANN	Yes, they were all yours here, in this house.

VINCENT	Cages of them – beautiful ones.
JENNIFER	(TO ANN) Yes, you used to talk about those.
ROBERT	I remember one in a cage out there. (POINTS TO THE CONSERVATORY)
ANN	We had them everywhere – the last one was the budgie that unfortunately … (STOPS)
JENNIFER	Did it die? The budgie?
ANN	Yes, it was actually Aisling's and it died.
ROBERT	That can be very traumatic. Was it sick?
ANN	A bit sick before it died. And then it died.
JENNIFER	I expect Aisling was devastated.
ANN	Yes, she was for a while.
DOROTHY	Of course because, as I discovered in life, death so often comes to those in whom we have invested so much love, trust and affection, leaving us empty and bereft.
JENNIFER	Yes. (TO ROBERT) Like our cat – Ginger.
ROBERT	Oh Ginger. Broke our hearts.
JENNIFER	It really did. But we never got another.
ROBERT	Couldn't, absolutely refused to, after Ginger.
ANN	(LIGHTLY) But the point is, we *did* have the budgies and they were all your idea, Larry, and they were beautiful.
JENNIFER	Exactly. Point well made, Ann.
ANN	(PLEASED) Thank you.
	PAUSE. THEN:
LARRY	Robert, how did you know we had a budgie in a cage out there? (THE CONSERVATORY)
ROBERT	What?
LARRY	You said you knew we had a budgie in a cage

	out there – how did you know that?
ROBERT	(LIGHTLY) A budgie in a cage? I never knew that.
LARRY	But you just said it.
ROBERT	I don't remember saying that.
ANN	I don't think he did, Larry.
LARRY	He said it just now. I heard him.
ROBERT	(LIGHTLY) But how would I know that, Larry? I was never here before, ever.
LARRY	Exactly – that's why I'm asking how you knew we had a budgie in our conservatory?
ANN	(LIGHTLY) Honestly, Larry – I don't remember Robert mentioning the conservatory at all.
LARRY	He didn't mention it – he pointed at it!
ROBERT	Pointed?
LARRY	Yes pointed at it. Like this! (POINTS)
ROBERT	I know how to point, Larry. But was I pointing at something else we were discussing?
LARRY	No you weren't – we were discussing the budgie in the cage and you said you knew about it and you pointed at it.
ROBERT	(LIGHTLY) At a budgie that wasn't there?
LARRY	That you said was there, in our conservatory.
ROBERT	That I couldn't have known about?
ANN	And I don't think he said it at all, Larry.
DOROTHY	I don't think he did either.
ANN	There, Larry – no one heard him.
LARRY	I shaggin' heard him!
ANN	Larry!

JENNIFER   I think I heard you saying it, Robert.

ROBERT   (ANGRILY) Oh really? (STANDS. POURS A WHISKEY) But how could you have heard me say it, Jennifer, when I couldn't have said it because I was never here so how could I have known?

LARRY   Except that you did say it.

ROBERT   (ANGRILY) But how could I – I was never here to know!

DOROTHY   But I was never here either and I know.

LARRY   You know what?

DOROTHY   Know you had a budgie out there – and I was never here.

JENNIFER   So how do you know, Dorothy?

DOROTHY   Because Ann told me all about that budgie.

ANN   (PANIC) What? No I didn't. I didn't tell anyone about all that.

DOROTHY   You did, Ann.

ANN   (NERVOUSLY) No I didn't. Honestly, Vincent.

DOROTHY   You told me how it was hanging out there, always singing, in its cage, in your conservatory, there. (POINTS)

ANN   (RELIEVED) Oh that it was out there, singing? – yes I told you that. (TO ALL) I told her that. Just that. I remember now.

DOROTHY   And that's how I knew it was there, without me ever being here.

JENNIFER   And do you know, Ann, you could have said it to me too.

ANN   I think I said it to everyone, I was always saying it – (POINTED) I think that's how everyone knew.

ROBERT   Then that must have been how I knew – so that's why I said it.

LARRY   But you just said you didn't say it.

ROBERT   But if everyone else says I said it then I may well have said it and I would have known because Ann told Jennifer and Jennifer told me. (DRINKS NERVOUSLY)

ANN   Yes, that must have been how it was.

ROBERT   Exactly. QED.

DOROTHY   And I really don't see why we are so concerned about who knew or didn't know about the budgie.

ROBERT   And neither do I.

LARRY   (TO ROBERT) Except that I saw you pointing.

ANN   Yes, and Larry, that has all been explained – that's the end of that!

JENNIFER   (LIGHTLY) Yes, and so concludes the mystery of who did or didn't see the budgie in the cage.

ANN   Yes. Everyone all right for more wine, water, sausage rolls? (EXHAUSTED) Help yourselves.

JENNIFER   Robert! Nothing more for you!

ROBERT   What?

JENNIFER   That's your fourth whiskey.

ROBERT   No, I … good God, you're right. Didn't notice. I'm back to the vino, Ann.

JENNIFER   (LIGHTLY) I think it may be a taxi home.

ROBERT   (ANNOYED) I'm fine, Jennifer. Honestly, I'm fine.

JENNIFER   A taxi. So, chat over – time to return to our Book Club and to recommence our second book reaction and analysis?

ANN   Yes!

DOROTHY   But a wonderful interruption, well worth

pausing for: seeing and hearing of Vincent's wonderful work.

ROBERT   Yes, magnificent accomplishments.

JENNIFER   And Larry, you will join us now?

LARRY   No, I don't think …

ANN   Oh Larry, yes – you loved this book, loved this story.

JENNIFER   Then you must, Larry.

ROBERT   Yes, Larry, come on – back up the men.

LARRY   No, I don't think …

VINCENT   Yes do, Larry – why not?

LARRY   (TO VINCENT) What?

VINCENT   I think you should. You've read the book, you know all about it, you have opinions on it.

DOROTHY   And then, for the first time, we will have a perfect balance: three men and three ladies.

ANN   Exactly. Say yes, Larry, please.

JENNIFER   Yes, make it a great Book Club evening, Larry.

ROBERT   Come on, Larry, support the men.

LARRY   Well, all right then.

JENNIFER   Excellent. Great. Wonderful. Thank you, Larry, thank you.

             A ROUND OF APPLAUSE, AS:

JENNIFER   (TO ANN) What a great Book Club.

ANN   (APPLAUDING) I'm so glad. Thank you, Larry.

ROBERT   I want to come to all of these.

JENNIFER   Application in writing please – signed by the bank manager! Yourself!

             LAUGHTER. THEN:

JENNIFER   And Vincent, as you are the new boy in our

	class ... sorry, club!
ROBERT	(MERRILY) Freudian!
JENNIFER	Club! – just to say that our modus operandi is that we first have what we call an immediate reaction, without interruption, from each member, followed by a more general analysis-slash-examination in which anything pertaining to the novel or its background or its author can be debated, dissected and discussed. So two parts – immediate reaction and then general discussion. All right, Vincent?
	VINCENT NODS.
JENNIFER	Any questions?
VINCENT	(QUIETLY) No – thank you very much.
ANN	(TO VINCENT) And we use the library for our ...
JENNIFER	Ann, I was thinking about that. We are all comfortable, so why not stay here?
ANN	Well ...?
ROBERT	I'm very settled here.
DOROTHY	Yes, it's very comfortable.
ANN	Larry?
LARRY	I don't care.
JENNIFER	Carried! – so here it will be. And Vincent, you know of course, that our book for discussion is Harper Lee's *To Kill a Mockingbird*?
VINCENT	Yes, I know.
JENNIFER	Good. Excellent. And important, everyone, as before, mobile phones, pagers, Blackberries all off and anyone for the loo or whatever, now please, and Robert, I am so anxious about your feet being so close to Notre Dame. Ann, could

we perhaps put it in …?

FROM NOW, JENNIFER WILL HURRIEDLY
COLLECT THE HARPER LEE BOOKS FROM THE
LIBRARY AND DISTRIBUTE THEM TO THE BOOK
CLUB HERE, ALL AS:

ANN   Of course. Maybe out in the conservatory for
           the time being. You don't mind, Vincent?

VINCENT   Oh no. (PICKING UP THE MODEL)

DOROTHY   (HELPING VINCENT) That would be nice,
           overlooking the garden.

ANN   Maybe we should bring more of them down
           here later – the cathedrals.

           VINCENT AND DOROTHY WILL CARRY NOTRE
           DAME MODEL TO THE CONSERVATORY AND
           RETURN, AS:

JENNIFER   (URGENTLY) Very good. Quickly now, please.
           And we have already begun this book before
           Vincent's most welcome arrival, so we can pick
           it up there – and, Robert, could you please
           switch to water or 7 Up or something?

ROBERT   I will. Soon. (POURS WINE) Ann, red for you?

ANN   What? Oh, I think half a glass won't do any
           harm – thank you, Robert. Larry, a drink?

LARRY   I have it here. (WITH THE WHISKEY BOTTLE)

ANN   That's Bushmills.

LARRY   I know what it is!

ANN   (ANNOYED) Oh whatever you like then. (SEES
           THAT ROBERT HAS ONLY HALF-FILLED HER
           GLASS. TO ROBERT) Keep going.

           DOROTHY AND VINCENT HAVE RETURNED
           FROM THE CONSERVATORY TO THEIR
           RESPECTIVE CHAIRS.

JENNIFER   Good, excellent – so please, everyone, settle down and we will now commence. (PAUSE) We have already had immediate reactions from Dorothy and Ann, both very positive and, for my immediate reaction, I would agree that the narrative has strength, the characters of Scout, Atticus and Boo Radley have depth and recognisability – although clearly lacking the metaphysical anguish of Virginia Woolf – and later on, I will be expressing some deeper reservations about the disappointingly sentimental, almost hillbilly, style of the writing of Harper Lee as she challenges the hegemonic forces of the time. Now, who will be next for immediate reaction? Robert?

ROBERT   Ok. Firstly, I must disagree completely on that last point – I love this book, read it many times, as much for its great story as for the excellent writing style of Harper Lee – I find that a major achievement for a girl … writing her first novel and at her tender age. Wonderful work, in my opinion, and mainly down to the beautiful writing style of Harper Lee.

JENNIFER   Interesting. Some points there for our general discussion. Now, who's next? Larry, do you have some opinions on this for your immediate reaction?

LARRY   What? Oh yes. (DRINKS. THEN) Well, just this one: no matter what you all think of the book and the way Harper Lee wrote it, the fact of the matter is that none of it matters because, in actual fact, the book wasn't written by her at all.

ROBERT   (AMUSED) What?

LARRY	(ANNOYED TO ROBERT) It wasn't written by Harper Lee – and with all your great talk and reading it over and over, you still don't know that she never wrote it.
ROBERT	Don't talk rubbish – of course she wrote it.
LARRY	(ANGRILY) It's not rubbish, she didn't write it!
DOROTHY	I think she did – it was hailed as an impressive literary debut.
ANN	Where did you get this, Larry?
ROBERT	Look, her name is on the front of the book and …
LARRY	Her name can be anywhere you like, but she didn't write it.
JENNIFER	Larry, of course she wrote it.
LARRY	No, she didn't!
ROBERT	(MERRILY) Then who wrote it? You?
JENNIFER	(LAUGHS) I don't think Larry is saying that.
ANN	(LAUGHS) No, I don't think so.
LARRY	(ANGRILY TOWARDS ANN) No I'm not saying that although I wouldn't be surprised, the way I'm now suddenly hearing about people writing books that never wrote books in their life before!
ANN	(ANNOYED) Larry, it's that whiskey you're hearing that from.
LARRY	No, Ann, it's not the whiskey – it's you yourself that told me about you suddenly writing books.
JENNIFER	What?
ROBERT	Are you writing a book, Ann?
ANN	No …

DOROTHY	Are you, Ann, really?
ANN	No I'm not!
LARRY	Oh are you not? – then what about the one about the fellow in the bedroom and on the stairs and in the wardrobe?
ROBERT	Well this is news.
LARRY	(TO ROBERT) Well, it shouldn't be to you!
ANN	(ANNOYED) Larry, you stop this at once!
LARRY	… seeing how the fellow in the book is named after you!
ROBERT	After me?
ANN	Larry, we are discussing Harper Lee here and not anyone else.
LARRY	Oh yes, very convenient, let's get off that subject and everything about you and the book and about him knowing how to point out where the budgie was.
ROBERT	What?
JENNIFER	(AUTHORITATIVELY) Stop, stop, will you all stop please! I have no idea where this is going but all we want at this point are immediate reactions to the book under discussion.
ANN	Exactly!
JENNIFER	But for now, can we just clarify this point about Harper Lee. Larry, Harper Lee did write *To Kill a Mockingbird*. Can we agree on that? (HOLDS UP THE BOOK) Look.
LARRY	And I'm telling you she didn't.
JENNIFER	She did!
LARRY	She didn't.
ROBERT	(MERRILY) You didn't write it, Ann, did you –

on the sly?

ANN   (SERIOUSLY) This is ridiculous!

JENNIFER   (PATIENTLY) Then, Larry – if she didn't, who
            are you saying did?

LARRY   (LOOKS TO VINCENT) Truman Capote.
            (PRONOUNCED AS IN 'BOAT')

VINCENT   (CORRECTLY) Truman Capote?

LARRY   Yes, him.

JENNIFER   Oh for God's sake, not this old chestnut.
            Larry, he didn't write it.

DOROTHY   His style is quite different, isn't it? He wrote
            In Cold Blood, *Breakfast at Tiffany's* …

JENNIFER   Exactly.

ANN   (EMBARRASSED) You must be mixing him up,
            Larry.

LARRY   I'm not, it was him that wrote it, not her, and
            he lived next door to her (TO VINCENT) didn't
            he? (TO ALL) … and that's how he wrote it for
            her and she put her name on it and she never
            wrote another book in her whole life, because
            she didn't write that one either.

ANN   (TO VINCENT) Did you tell him this?

VINCENT   What?

LARRY   No he didn't and I don't need to be told things
            – I found this out myself.

JENNIFER   Listen Larry, that theory was discredited years
            ago – nobody believes that anymore.

LARRY   Well they should because it's true!

JENNIFER   (PATIENTLY) Ok, and what else is true – that
            Christopher Marlowe wrote *Hamlet*, Zelda
            Fitzgerald wrote *The Great Gatsby* and Clint
            Eastwood is the son of Stan Laurel?

ROBERT	He's his son? Is he?!
JENNIFER	No he's not!
ROBERT	Is Stan Laurel the fat one or the skinny one?
JENNIFER	(ANNOYED) It doesn't matter which he is because it's not true! – no more than Truman Capote wrote *To Kill a Mockingbird*!
LARRY	(ANNOYED) Except that he did and he let Harper Lee put her name on it and she never wrote another book in her whole life!
ROBERT	Larry, with all due respects, you are now talking through your arse again …
LARRY	(ANGRILY) No I am not!
ROBERT	… and, typical of you, all that is coming out is total crap!
LARRY	(JUMPS TO HIS FEET. KNOCKS OVER A CHAIR. FURIOUSLY) It is not total crap, no more than all these stories I've been hearing about you is total crap – and I'm not an eejit and you can drag me through the courts if you want to squeeze me for every penny we haven't got, but I'm not letting you away with all you've been up to in here: pointing out the budgie and then going all innocent and she (ANN) backing you up …
ROBERT	(TO ALL) What is he drinking?
LARRY	… and whatever you were doing in the wardrobes and on the stairs and in every other part of the house that we don't know about …
ANN	(FURIOUSLY) Larry, will you shut up!
LARRY	… and another thing, and deny it if you like, but if you ever put a hand near my daughter or her friend in the private office of that bank of yours …
ROBERT	Now you hold on!

LARRY	No, *you* hold on because I swear to Christ I'll do twenty years for you if you as much as touched my young one …
ROBERT	And you better have proof of what you're saying because I have witnesses here …
LARRY	Oh I have proof! I have proof!
ANN	No you haven't!
JENNIFER	What is all this?!
ROBERT	Right! Let's have the proof, let's have it now!
LARRY	I know you, I know you – two temporary girls working down in your bank …
ROBERT	You say that once more, without proof, and I'll have you jailed for slander …
LARRY	The proof is what my daughter told me …
ANN	But she didn't tell you!
JENNIFER	(TO ROBERT) Told him what? What did she tell him?
ROBERT	(TO JENNIFER) Told him nothing!
LARRY	(TO JENNIFER) It wasn't nothing.
JENNIFER	(FURIOUSLY TO ROBERT) Oh my God, is this Mandy Ryan all over again, is it?
ROBERT	No it's not, it's not and he has no proof.
JENNIFER	(FURIOUSLY) Oh Jesus Christ!
LARRY	I have proof – and the other proof of the other thing is you pointing at the budgie.
ROBERT	(TO JENNIFER) Listen to him! (TO LARRY) What budgie? There's no budgie!
LARRY	The budgie and you and my wife in here when I was down in Wexford.
ANN	That is not true – and shut up Larry!
DOROTHY	(LOUDLY) Gentlemen please! – this is a Book Club!

ROBERT	(TO JENNIFER) See? He has no proof of anything …
JENNIFER	(DESPAIR) I do not believe this!
ROBERT	(TO LARRY) But we have enough proof here tonight that you're a bullshitter, a crap-talker, a failure and bankrupt …
LARRY	And you're a liar and a whoremaster …
ROBERT	You're just an ignorant drunk, raving about the first things that come into your empty head, pointing at budgies that aren't there!
VINCENT	(SUDDENLY ON HIS FEET, ANGRY AND LOUD) He's not raving – he's telling the truth and I'll tell you now about that budgie.
ROBERT	Well, look who's joining in! I know all about you!
VINCENT	And I know all about you!
LARRY	(LOUDLY) Stay out of it, Vincent.
VINCENT	(TO ROBERT) I know you for what you are.
ROBERT	(TO VINCENT) And do you think we don't all know what you were in jail for?
ANN	Stop! Please stop!
VINCENT	You say one more thing about me and …
ROBERT	… trying to castrate a man who was innocent …
VINCENT	He wasn't innocent! I knew what he was doing!
ROBERT	He was innocent and he died innocent and you went to jail!
LARRY	Miscarriage of justice!
ROBERT	Miscarriage my arse – I read it all on Google, it's all on the Internet.
VINCENT	You're going too far, my friend!
ROBERT	No I'm not, I can say more, I Googled it up!

LARRY	I'll Google you up – you've been asking for this! (RUNS TOWARDS ROBERT)
ANN	(HOLDS LARRY) Stop, Larry – stop!
ROBERT	(MOVES AWAY) … and then back here with his churches and your budgies and your accusations and his matchstick cathedrals!
VINCENT	(ANGRY BUT SOFTER) All right, I'll tell you now about that budgie (POINTING TO THE CONSERVATORY) – because I killed it, I killed Aisling's budgie with my own hands.
ROBERT	What?
JENNIFER	(AGHAST) You killed it?
VINCENT	I crushed it to death in my fist.
DOROTHY	In the heat of the moment!
VINCENT	I was holding it in my hand …
ANN	Don't!
VINCENT	… and she began to tell me about you in that bank of yours and what you were doing!
JENNIFER	Oh my God!
LARRY	(TO VINCENT) She told you too?
ROBERT	She told him nothing, Jennifer.
VINCENT	She told me enough.
JENNIFER	(FURIOUSLY) You bastard, Robert!
ROBERT	(ANGRILY) No Jennifer, I did nothing! (TO VINCENT) And you're a liar …
LARRY	She told both of us.
ANN	She didn't tell you, Larry! (TO VINCENT) What exactly did she tell you, Vincent?
VINCENT	She told me enough and she only eighteen, an innocent girl …
ROBERT	She couldn't have told you or she's a liar too!

LARRY	We're all liars, are we? – well, I've heard enough … (RUNS AT ROBERT) you bastard, pervert, whoremaster!
ANN	No, Larry!
ROBERT	(MOVES) Lunatics. You're all lunatics!
	ROBERT TURNS TOWARDS THE ENTRANCE DOOR – BUT LARRY STANDS IN HIS WAY. ROBERT TURNS AND RUNS TOWARDS THE CONSERVATORY, BUT VINCENT BLOCKS HIS WAY. VINCENT HAS TAKEN THE KNIFE FROM HIS MODEL TOOL-KIT BOX. ALL THIS AS:
DOROTHY	He has a knife! He has a knife! (RUNS INTO THE LIBRARY, CLOSING THE DOOR)
VINCENT	(BLOCKING ROBERT'S ESCAPE TO THE CONSERVATORY) Not so fast.
ROBERT	(HITS VINCENT. RUNS TO THE LIBRARY) I did nothing!
VINCENT	(FALLING) Get him!
ANN	(HOLDS LARRY) No, Larry!
LARRY	(STRUGGLING) Let me go!
JENNIFER	For God's sake – will you all just sit down!
ROBERT	(AT THE LIBRARY DOOR, WHICH IS LOCKED FROM THE INSIDE BY DOROTHY) Let me in! Let me in!
LARRY	(HELD BY ANN) Ah – she's locked it!
ROBERT	(PANIC) Let me in, you bitch!
VINCENT	(SHOWING HIS CUT HAND) Blood! I fell on my knife!
ROBERT	(SHOUTS) Open the door, open the fucking door!
LARRY	(SHAKES FREE OF ANN) Now we have you. (RUNS AT ROBERT)

> ROBERT EXPERTLY TAKES LARRY'S RUN, SPINS HIM AROUND AND HOLDS HIS HEAD IN A STRONG HEADLOCK.

LARRY (IN PAIN) My neck!

ROBERT Don't move anyone or I'll break his neck! Jennifer! Get the police! Your mobile!

JENNIFER What?

ROBERT Get the fucking police!

JENNIFER Yes. Right. (FINDS HER MOBILE)

LARRY My neck!

ANN Don't hurt him! Please don't hurt him!

ROBERT (TO LARRY) Tell him (VINCENT) not to come near me with that knife.

LARRY (TO VINCENT) Don't! My neck!

ROBERT (TO JENNIFER) Nine … nine … nine.

JENNIFER (DIALLING) I know!

VINCENT (WRAPPING A HANDKERCHIEF AROUND HIS BLEEDING HAND) No police! I said no police!

ANN Oh don't Jennifer, not the police.

VINCENT (TO ROBERT) You let him go now or you'll be singing soprano for the rest of your life.

JENNIFER (INTO PHONE) Police – quick, quick.

ROBERT (PANIC) Any one of you move, anyone, and his neck is broken. I know how to do it, I am trained to do this and I will! (KICKS THE LIBRARY DOOR) Open the door, you stupid bitch!

VINCENT He won't do it. (MOVES. MENACINGLY TO ROBERT) Come on.

LARRY (GASPS AT VINCENT) Don't move.

ROBERT (KICKS THE DOOR) Open it!

JENNIFER	(INTO MOBILE) Hello?
ROBERT	Tell them to get here now!
JENNIFER	(INTO MOBILE, ANXIOUSLY) Hello, police? – we're having our Book Club meeting here … and someone wants to castrate my husband! (LISTENS)
ROBERT	Stop saying that!
VINCENT	(ANGUISHED – ALMOST LIKE A CAGED ANIMAL) Jesus Christ, I'll do it now – I'm going back to jail now anyway. I can do it!
ANN	(HARD) Vincent, don't move!
ROBERT	Give them the address, you stupid bitch!
JENNIFER	(FURIOUSLY) Don't you dare call me that!
ROBERT	Give them the fucking address!
JENNIFER	(TO ANN) What's this address – street or road?
ANN	Just ring off. Vincent, put that knife away.
VINCENT	No! And I'm coming!
LARRY	He's breaking my neck!
	SUDDENLY, THE HOUSE PHONE RINGS.
ANN	(LOUD AND STRONG) Stop! Everybody stop! The phone! That could be Aisling!
VINCENT	(STOPS) Aisling? How do you know?
	AS THE PHONE RINGS, ANN HAS RUN TO THE COMPUTER, MOVED THE MOUSE AND PRESSED SOME KEYS. THE SITE APPEARS ON THE PLASMA SCREEN. SHE RUNS TO THE PHONE, ALL AS:
ANN	She said she might be on to us and we can ask her. Jennifer, we can ask her.
JENNIFER	(INTO MOBILE) Just a second, garda.
ANN	Larry, Vincent, don't move.
LARRY	I can't move anyway!

ANN	(PICKS UP THE PHONE) Hello? (BRIGHTLY) Ah Aisling, great to hear from you ... (LISTENS) Yes, we're online, love. Yes, now. Ok. (SLAMS THE PHONE DOWN. RUNS TO THE COMPUTER) Quiet everyone now.
ROBERT	Is that a webcam?
ANN	Just be quiet please, everyone! And nobody in vision with the camera! Move!
	EVERYONE SHUFFLES OUT OF VISION OF THE CAMERA, STILL HOLDING THEIR DEFENSIVE/ AGGRESSIVE POSITIONS.
ANN	Ok – I'll be talking to her on the television, so quiet! (PRESSES A KEY)
	SUDDENLY AISLING APPEARS ON THE PLASMA SCREEN. SHE IS IN A GOOD MOOD.
AISLING	Hello Mum? Mum?
JENNIFER	(QUIETLY INTO HER MOBILE) Everything's all right – we are all going to talk to the television. (POWERS OFF)
ANN	(HARD) Quiet!
AISLING	Hello Mum? Dad?
	EVERYONE FREEZES AS ANN MOVES INTO THE VISION OF THE CAMERA.
ANN	Hello love, here I am. Is everything all right with you?
AISLING	Yes Mum. Is your Book Club still on or ...?
ANN	Yes, it's on, love – on here now.
AISLING	In the library room?
ANN	What? Yes, in the library. I just came out.
	A GROAN OF PAIN FROM LARRY IN ROBERT'S HEADLOCK.

AISLING   Who's there? Is Dad there?

LARRY   (GASPS) I can't breathe.

JENNIFER   (WHISPERS) Let his neck go!

ROBERT   (WHISPERS) In my arse!

AISLING   Mum, what's all that? Is Dad there or not?
              Who *is* there?

ANN   Oh just some of the group who came out,
              discussing the book.

LARRY   (TRYING) Yes love, Dad here. (ANGRILY) I
              can't breathe!

AISLING   I can't see you, Dad.

              ANN ANGRILY TAKES CONTROL – HURRIES TO
              WHERE ROBERT HOLDS LARRY AND VINCENT
              THREATENS WITH HIS KNIFE.

ANN   (HARD WHISPER) Vincent, get back! Back! (TO
              ROBERT) Let go of his neck now!

ROBERT   (WHISPERS) Not until ... (INDICATES
              VINCENT)

ANN   (TO VINCENT) Back further! (TO ROBERT)
              Now – and we'll hear what she has to say!

              VINCENT HAS RETREATED. ROBERT RELEASES
              LARRY. ANN RETURNS TO THE COMPUTER, AS:

AISLING   Dad, what's going on?

LARRY   (RELIEVED) It's all right, love – we're just
              reading and talking. But there's something
              your mother wants to ...

ANN   It's all right, love, just a little question for you.

AISLING   But where is Dad?

ANN   He's there, darling. And everything is all right
              with you, is it?

AISLING   (ANNOYED) For God's sake – yes! It's just

	that I was talking to him earlier and I said something that he might have picked up all wrong about Mr Travers in the bank and me and Sarah and Uncle Vincent and …
ROBERT	(ANXIOUSLY CALLS) Aisling, this is Robert Travers here – I'd just like to know …
ANN	(TO ROBERT) Quiet!
AISLING	(ANGRILY) Jesus Christ – is Mr Travers there listening to me? Is everyone listening? Holy shit – who *is* there?!
ANN	Aisling, your language – you never used …
AISLING	Who's there, Mum? Dad and Mr Travers and who else? Is Dorothy there, is Jennifer there?
ANN	No, Dorothy is still in the library …
JENNIFER	I'm here, Aisling – how are you, pet?
ROBERT	Christ! Just ask her!
VINCENT	(WITH HIS KNIFE, QUIETLY TO ROBERT) Yes, and as soon as …
ANN	(LOUDLY TO AISLING) Yes, that's who is here, love – and your dad just wants to know what exactly you meant when you last spoke to him.
AISLING	(ANGRILY) I knew it! I just knew it! I knew he got it all wrong!
LARRY	Aisling, I got nothing wrong …
VINCENT	(CALLS) And you said it to me too, Aisling!
AISLING	Jesus Christ – is Uncle Vincent there too?
ANN	Yes but …
AISLING	(FURIOUS) I just knew this was going to happen – I knew as soon as I said what *didn't* happen that you'd all freak out, all thinking that it *did* happen – it's no wonder I was driven out of my head in that fucking house

	with all your suspicions and questions and expectations …
LARRY	No Aisling, you said to me …
VINCENT	And you also told me it happened, Aisling!
AISLING	(FURIOUSLY) For Christ sake, Uncle Vincent, I didn't – I was trying to tell you, in case you heard the rumours about Mr Travers …
ROBERT	What rumours?
AISLING	… because I knew if you heard the rumours I knew it'd be like what happened to you in England – but you heard half of what I was saying and you lost the head and closed your fist and crushed my budgie to death before I could finish what I was fucking trying to tell you!
ANN	Aisling, your language …
AISLING	(SOBBING AND ANGRY) And I loved that budgie, that budgie was all I had and I loved it more than anything else in this world …
ANN	Stop it, Aisling!
AISLING	No Mum, I loved it and he crushed it to death in front of me.
VINCENT	Because I thought you were telling me …
AISLING	You thought! You thought! You wouldn't listen and you still won't!
ROBERT	Aisling, will you just tell them what happened in the bank when …
AISLING	(SHOUTS) For God's sake – nothing happened!
LARRY	But you said Sarah …
AISLING	Dad, I'm not responsible for Sarah …
JENNIFER	Aisling, did Sarah say that Robert …?

AISLING	Sarah is a spoofer, I don't know what she said about Mr Travers or me or her …
ROBERT	But the fact is that nothing happened between me and her, did it, Aisling?
AISLING	How would I know that? – but one thing I do know, Mr Travers: nothing happened between you and me, no matter what Sarah or anyone said or didn't say.
ROBERT	At last! Thank you, Aisling!
AISLING	(ANGRILY) And I'll tell you why – because in that bank I didn't exist, did I? – when did you ever talk to me or say good morning to me …?
ROBERT	Aisling!
AISLING	… or even say my name! – I wasn't Sarah, was I? – I wasn't pretty like Sarah or sexy like Sarah …
ROBERT	Now wait a minute.
AISLING	To you I was her invisible friend, the plain one, the one with nothing to say, with few friends …
ANN	Stop, Aisling! – you are very pretty, you have lots of friends that you love and who love you …
AISLING	Mum, I know what I am – but I'll tell you who I *did* love: I loved that budgie, I loved it more than any of you can ever imagine and that lunatic killed it before my eyes!
VINCENT	Aisling, I …
AISLING	But ok ok, that's all in the past, Mum – I am out here now, away from it all …
ANN	Yes Aisling and we hope you are safe and eating well and we want you to come home to us …

AISLING   (CONTINUING) … and I'm not worried anymore, really I'm not, because I've now said my say, the silent one has spoken and now you can all do whatever you like because, here, the sky is blue, the sun is up, it's a beautiful day and we are all off to the beach on the bikes …

ANN   Aisling, listen to me now …

AISLING   Sorry Mum, I really got to go … (TO SOMEONE OFF, MERRILY) What? Oh yes, almost forgot.

ANN   Who is with you there, Aisling?

AISLING   (TO THE CAMERA). And Mum, Dad, just one thing – please don't worry about me anymore because I'm no longer worrying about you – (MERRILY) and just in case you are getting the wrong impression, *again*! – yes, we are all going to the ocean now and yes we will be riding like mad on the beach, on motorcycles! Look! (PUTS ON A CRASH HELMET. LAUGHTER OFF) Love you Mum, love you, Dad. (MERRILY TO OFF) It doesn't fit! (LAUGHS)

    AISLING CLOSES DOWN, THE SCREEN REVERTS TO THE WEBCAM SITE AND TO BLACK. SILENCE. EVERYONE SOMBRE AND SUBDUED. BUT ROBERT QUIETLY, VERY ANGRY.

ANN   I apologise to everyone – I have no idea what kind of company she's keeping out there …

JENNIFER   Quite all right, Ann. It's the age she's at.

    THE LIBRARY DOOR SLOWLY OPENS AND DOROTHY TENTATIVELY EMERGES.

DOROTHY   Is it all over?

ANN   Yes – are you all right, Dorothy?

ROBERT   (MIMICS) Yes, are you all right, Dorothy?

	(ANGRILY) Why did you lock that door? I was about to be knifed by that lunatic. (VINCENT)
VINCENT	(QUIETLY) I was acting in good faith because …
ROBERT	Good faith?!
LARRY	(TOWARDS ANN) And, by the way, that's not the only issue here.
ROBERT	Oh there's more is there? (TO VINCENT) And is there more from you too: more judgements, more accusations, more questions …?
JENNIFER	(LOUDER) Well, the only question I have for you is – how old is this Sarah girl?
ROBERT	(TO VINCENT AND LARRY) See?
JENNIFER	Nothing changes, Robert, does it?
ROBERT	Jennifer, what do you want me to say?
JENNIFER	(FURIOUSLY) Nothing! Because you have never changed.
ROBERT	God's sake! These are lies! What do you want me to do?
DOROTHY	(LOUDLY) Well I would like you to stop shouting!
ROBERT	Well I won't! – because it is you who has me like this!
DOROTHY	My doctor says that shouting …
ROBERT	(FURIOUS) Ah you and your doctor – go and tell your doctor that your only problem is that you are too spoiled, with too much money that was handed to you for doing nothing and now you get too much attention and, when you don't get it, you know exactly how to screw everybody until you do get it. I know your type!

DOROTHY   How dare you!

JENNIFER   Robert, will you shut up!

ROBERT   No, we're all on to her down at the bank. (TO DOROTHY) And you may as well know that nobody believes about all those people dying on you ...

DOROTHY   My sister died ...

ROBERT   And nobody believes that either – just because everyone died on Virginia Woolf doesn't mean they all died on you too! Get real!

JENNIFER   Robert!

VINCENT   (SUDDENLY ANGRY) And I think that's about enough of your bullying a defenceless lady with your accusations ...

ANN   Please, everybody!

ROBERT   (TO VINCENT) *My* accusations? Have you any idea what your accusations could do to my life, my marriage, my reputation, my future ...

VINCENT   If you are innocent you have nothing ...

ROBERT   ... how years of work can be destroyed in just a second? You don't see that, do you not? No you don't! Ok, I'll show you – let me give you a simple example ... (GOES QUICKLY TO THE CONSERVATORY)

JENNIFER   No, Robert, no!

ROBERT   (OFF) ... let me give you just a little indication of the impact of what you can do with all your scurrilous talk ...

A CRASH OF WOOD IS HEARD, OFF. ROBERT WALKS IN. THE MATCHSTICK MODEL IS STILL ON HIS FOOT WHERE HE HAS STAMPED ON IT.

LARRY   Oh Jesus – he's after putting his boot through

Notre Dame!

ROBERT   (TO VINCENT) In your case, it'd be a bit like this – except that you could fix this with a few matchsticks and a bit of glue but my life could be ruined forever, thanks to you! (TO ALL) Let's all think about that, let's all keep that in mind as we now continue with this great Book Club evening!

BLACKOUT.

END OF SCENE 1, ACT 2

Act 2, Scene 2

It is fifteen minutes later. Robert is drinking coffee, clearly depressed. Vincent is examining his broken model. Larry sits quietly. Ann is pouring coffee and setting out biscuits. Jennifer is speaking on her mobile, very upbeat. Dorothy is off, outside in her car.

JENNIFER   (INTO MOBILE) Yes Sheila, we should all check diaries for Wednesday the fifteenth and network our availability, Ok? (LISTENS) Excellent. Yes, this evening was really good, you would have loved it – Ann did us proud and great debates on both *Lighthouse* and *Mockingbird* – so don't miss the next one. (LISTENS) What? Oh no – no, it's Monica's choice. *Atonement*. All right. That's great, see you then. Bye. Bye Sheila (POWERS OFF) Now, there we are and, as we are agreed, nobody need be any the wiser of what happened here.

ANN   Agreed.

ROBERT   Some hope.

JENNIFER   And it all happened because some people are inherently stupid and don't know how to stop drinking.

ANN   I'm so sorry, Jennifer.

JENNIFER   No, not you, Ann – you gave us a wonderful evening. Others, however, seemed determined to destroy not only themselves, but everyone else around them.

ROBERT   For God's sake, I apologised didn't I?

JENNIFER   Did you apologise to Vincent for destroying his beautiful work?

ROBERT   Did he apologise to me?

JENNIFER   And to Dorothy? Or are you still intent on having yourself either demoted and, at worst, sacked for your incredible stupidity?

ROBERT   I apologised to her!

JENNIFER   Well, we are not leaving here until you do it again, and mean it!

ROBERT   (ANGRILY) I'll do it again if you want! Where is she anyway?

ANN   She went out to her car to get something. Drink your coffee, Jennifer, and some biscuits here too.

JENNIFER   Thank you, Ann, I'm fine. Vincent, can it be repaired, do you think?

VINCENT   (EXAMINING IT) May not bother.

ANN   (SWEETLY) Larry, your coffee is there ... and some biscuits.

LARRY   (GRUMPILY) Don't want any. And let me tell you, that other excuse of yours cuts no ice with me, that cock-and-bull story about you writing ...

ANN   (HARD AND QUIET) Not again and not now!

            JENNIFER'S MOBILE RINGS

JENNIFER   (ANGRILY TO HERSELF) Soon as I turn it on! (INTO MOBILE) Hello? Oh, the gardaí? Yes, guard, that was me.

VINCENT   (CONCERNED) The police?

JENNIFER   (INTO MOBILE) Yes, oh yes, I am so sorry ... (LISTENS) ... Yes, I was speaking to a male colleague of yours and ... (LISTENS) ... yes, absolutely and we are so ... (LISTENS) ... yes, a Book Club ... (LISTENS) ... yes, ehhh, *To the Lighthouse* and *To Kill a Mockingbird* ... (LISTENS) ... no no no, his style is quite different – it was definitely Harper Lee ... (LISTENS) ... yes and so sorry ... yes, thank you ... yes good evening. (POWERS OFF) Hopefully, the end of that.

VINCENT   (RELIEVED) Thank God.

THE DOOR OPENS. DOROTHY COMES IN. SHE CARRIES A SMALL PHOTO ALBUM.

ANN   Ah Dorothy – I have some coffee here and biscuits ...

DOROTHY   No thank you, Ann – I am going quite soon ...

JENNIFER   As are we, Dorothy.

DOROTHY   Well, before you do – (TO ROBERT) Mr Travers, I have been searching my car for this little photograph album.

ROBERT   Robert, Dorothy, please.

DOROTHY   It is to show you some photos of (INDICATES) my sisters, my cousin, my friend in Paris, my chiropractor ...

ROBERT   Oh yes, of course, thank you, very nice, excellent.

DOROTHY   This is my late sister that you didn't believe ever existed.

ROBERT   I apologised, Dorothy, and I see her now.

DOROTHY   Are you familiar with the biblical quotation 'Blessed are those who have not seen and have believed'?

ROBERT   Yes, I think so.

DOROTHY   Good. Then you will know why I shall be making arrangements to terminate all my business at your bank and transfer it elsewhere.

JENNIFER   (QUIETLY) Oh Jesus Christ!

ROBERT   Now hold on a minute, Dorothy – you can't just …

DOROTHY   Thank you, Mr Travers.

ROBERT   (HARDER) For heaven's sake, why would you want to …?

JENNIFER   (STANDING) All right Robert, you say no more now, thank you. Ann, we are going.

ROBERT   (HARD) Well, firstly, I haven't finished my coffee.

JENNIFER   Leave your coffee. Dorothy, could I please ask you not to be hasty in this?

DOROTHY   I am closing all my accounts and portfolios, Jennifer. My decision is final.

JENNIFER   Very well. (TO ROBERT) Idiot. (TO ANN, SWEETLY) Thank you, Ann – that was a fascinating evening.

ANN   Jennifer, I am so sorry …

JENNIFER   No no, thank you so much. Goodbye Larry, Vincent – and Dorothy, please sleep on that before you do anything. Please! Thank you.

ANN   I'll see you out, Jennifer.

JENNIFER   (AS SHE GOES) Thank you, Ann. (HARDER) And one thing for certain – in future, it will just be us girls. No one else. No one!

ANN   Definitely.

           ANN AND JENNIFER GO. ROBERT SLOWLY FINISHES HIS COFFEE.

ROBERT   (STANDS TO GO) Right. I think I have made my point. Vincent, good luck with your life

... and everything. And Larry, just this: I now think it would be best for us to meet, with our legal boys, very soon, for some straight talking ...

JENNIFER (OFF) Robert! Keys of the car – now!

ROBERT God's sake! (CALLS) Right! (QUIET AND HARD TO LARRY) Because, I am sorry to say, the gloves are now off – so let's make that meeting first thing Monday morning and let's have your call to confirm that tomorrow, no later. The sooner you settle this up the better for you, while you still have some options. (TURNS TO LOOK AT DOROTHY)

JENNIFER (OFF. LOUDLY) Robert!!

ROBERT (ANGRILY) Coming! Coming!

ROBERT GOES QUICKLY.

VINCENT (WITH NOTRE DAME) I'll put this upstairs.

LARRY It's all right where it is, Vincent.

VINCENT No, it looks bad here, in that state.

VINCENT GOES WITH HIS BROKEN MODEL.

DOROTHY (OF THE ALBUM) These really are my family and friends.

LARRY Of course they are – Bosnia and all.

DOROTHY Bolivia.

LARRY Bolivia, of course.

A CAR HORN AND ACCELERATED CRUNCH OF WHEELS ON GRAVEL AS JENNIFER AND ROBERT DRIVE OFF.

LARRY God Almighty, do you hear that? – there'll be tracks inches deep in my gravel. (GOES TO THE CONSERVATORY)

DOROTHY I hope I didn't do that too.

LARRY   (COMING THROUGH WITH A GARDEN RAKE) No, you drive normally – but he did that deliberately coming in and now she's doing it going out!

             LARRY PASSES ANN AS SHE COMES BACK IN.

LARRY   (TO ANN) The pair of them think they're on *Top Gear* or something.

             LARRY GOES WITH THE GARDEN RAKE. ANN AND DOROTHY ALONE. COMFORTABLE.

ANN   God – what an evening.

DOROTHY   The men didn't fit in.

ANN   (CONSIDERS) True.

DOROTHY   Men always fight.

ANN   Yes they do. (PAUSE) Dorothy, Jennifer is very worried about ... I mean, will you really move your accounts because Jennifer says Robert got his promotion on the strength of securing your investments and if they begin to downsize at the bank ...

DOROTHY   Well, it depends on how his meeting goes with Larry.

ANN   With Larry?

DOROTHY   They are meeting on Monday. If he is ... kind and conciliatory to Larry, I may leave my accounts as they are.

ANN   Oh Dorothy, that would be great, that would be such a relief. I can secretly tell Jennifer to gently tell Robert to be ... conciliatory ... and I won't say a word to Larry in case they start to lock horns again ...

DOROTHY   Ann, I'm not doing it for Larry. I'm doing it for you.

ANN   For me?

DOROTHY   You really don't remember our conversation
           in the car, do you? – on our way home from
           Monica's?

ANN   When I told you too much about ...

DOROTHY   And I told you a great deal about me, and my
           life ... and why I admire Virginia Woolf so
           much?

ANN   No, I honestly don't remember ...

DOROTHY   No matter – you listened, as you always do and
           you were kind, very kind, so thank you. Now I
           really should be going. (STANDS)

           THE DOOR OPENS. VINCENT COMES IN.
           HE CARRIES AN ENVELOPE AND A SMALL
           BIRDCAGE, MADE OF MATCHSTICKS, WITH ITS
           DOOR PERMANENTLY OPEN. HE CONCEALS
           THIS BEHIND HIS BACK, AS:

VINCENT   Ah just in time – you are leaving?

DOROTHY   Yes Vincent – enough of books for one
           evening.

VINCENT   Because you liked my work, a present for you.
           (HE REVEALS IT)

DOROTHY   (DELIGHTED) A birdcage. How lovely. You
           made it of course?

VINCENT   A long time ago. With its door open and the
           lock on the inside ...

DOROTHY   (LOOKING) How intriguing.

VINCENT   ... maybe to pretend that we have the
           wherewithal to be free?

DOROTHY   Indeed. Thank you.

VINCENT   And a surprise for you, Ann. (THE ENVELOPE)

ANN   I love surprises. Let me see.

VINCENT	Later. Open it later. Everything is for later – when, hopefully, all is forgotten and all is forgiven and we are at peace again. Later. (AS HE GOES) Goodbye Dorothy.
DOROTHY	Goodbye Vincent. Perhaps I'll see you going down for your paper sometime?
VINCENT	I go every morning.
DOROTHY	I know you do.
VINCENT	(PLEASED) Good.
	VINCENT GOES QUICKLY. ANN LOOKS AT DOROTHY AND PULLS THE ENVELOPE OPEN. SHE TAKES OUT A BLACK BOOK.
ANN	My diary! It's my diary!
DOROTHY	Is that the one in which you wrote …?
ANN	(FLICKING THROUGH THE PAGES) That I thought Aisling had taken – but how did Vincent have it? Where did he get it? Did he read the … oh my God.
DOROTHY	Well, perhaps best not to ask the questions.
ANN	(CONFUSED. UNSURE) Maybe.
DOROTHY	And perhaps that was his message just now – about all been forgiven and everyone at peace?
ANN	Oh I don't know – but thank God anyway. It will be destroyed this very night!
DOROTHY	Good. Now, I will see you at our next Book Club on the fifteenth?
ANN	Of course. A more relaxed one.
DOROTHY	And thank you so much for this one.
	THEY HUG FAREWELL, AS LARRY COMES IN.
LARRY	Ah, you're off, Dorothy – I'll guide you out – you have a very tricky reverse there.

DOROTHY   Thank you, Larry. I will be careful with your gravel.

LARRY   I have the rake outside anyway.

ANN   Safe home, Dorothy.

DOROTHY   Thank you, Ann. (TO LARRY, AS SHE GOES) Vincent gave me a birdcage.

LARRY   Oh lovely.

THEY ARE GONE. ANN QUICKLY LOOKS AT HER DIARY – AT THE RELEVANT ENTRIES.

ANN   (TO HERSELF) Oh God – oh my God! (HORRIFIED) What was I thinking of!

OUTSIDE, DOROTHY'S CAR IS HEARD GOING. ANN LOOKS AROUND FOR A PLACE TO HIDE THE DIARY. SHE PUTS IT UNDER A CUSHION ON A CHAIR AND STANDS NONCHALANTLY AS LARRY COMES IN WITH THE RAKE. HE WILL GO TO THE CONSERVATORY AS:

LARRY   (GRUMPILY) Never saw anything like it – gravel and pebbles everywhere, up onto the porch, on the mat, in the grass, stones that'd destroy a lawnmower …

ANN   From Dorothy too?

LARRY   (COMING FROM THE CONSERVATORY) No, the other pair. No thought for anyone. And on Monday I have to go in and see him – he gave me the ultimatum – no more avoiding him anymore, time to face the music and, after tonight, I think we all know how that'll be.

ANN   There's still some coffee here if you … (POURING)

LARRY   It's not coffee I want.

ANN   It's poured now anyway.

BEFORE ANN CAN MOVE, LARRY HAS SAT
HEAVILY INTO THE CHAIR, ONTO THE CUSHION
THAT HIDES THE DIARY. SHE REALISES THIS
IN HORROR, BUT STAYS CALM AS SHE PUTS
HIS COFFEE ASIDE AND CHOOSES ANOTHER
CHAIR AND WATCHES IN TREPIDATION. ALL
AS:

LARRY   And you may as well know, we may as well
          face it – this could be the end of everything:
          we'll have to start letting things go, lucky if
          we have a roof over our heads at the wind-
          up because, once that fellow gets going,
          he'll throw the book at me ... (MOVES
          UNCOMFORTABLY IN THE CHAIR, ADJUSTING
          THE CUSHION) ... and that bank will show no
          mercy, they never do – he made that bloody
          clear to me tonight.

ANN   (HOPEFULLY) Well, you never know.

LARRY   The point is I bloody well *do* know. And
          another thing: I'm going to find out about
          this diary of yours and your story about a book
          you're supposed to be writing ...

ANN   (WEAKLY) Larry, I have already explained ...

LARRY   (ADJUSTING THE CUSHION FOR MORE
          COMFORT) Oh I know, but now I intend to
          find out the truth – and the next time Aisling
          is on, I'm going to tell her to send that diary
          over to me, to *me*, Ann, by registered post,
          because I want to see the proof of how you
          suddenly wanted to write a book and how
          you were going to go about it. I want to see all
          that, with my own eyes, in this diary of yours.
          (MOVES UNCOMFORTABLY)

ANN   (ANXIOUSLY) Well do whatever you want –
          but I think I've heard enough of all that for

one night – I'm too tired and exhausted now and all I want to do is close my eyes, so maybe you'd turn off that computer and I can get some peace at last.

LARRY   Me?

ANN   (CLOSES HER EYES) Just press the green lit-up button on the front.

LARRY   (STANDS AND GOES) As if I'm not exhausted too, after all I've been put through.

LARRY GOES TO THE COMPUTER AND TURNS IT OFF. AS HE DOES, ANN TAKES THE OPPORTU-NITY TO CROSS TO HIS CHAIR AND SIT. LARRY TURNS.

LARRY   Why did you move? That was my chair.

ANN   This one is more comfortable.

LARRY   Not any more comfortable than the one you were in.

ANN   Well I'm not getting into another argument about that – (NOW CONFIDENT) but let me say this: that I'd be delighted if you got my diary sent over to you, by registered post …

LARRY   Oh I will, don't worry.

ANN   … because then you will see – as I am tired telling you! – how, on each page, as clear as daylight, I wrote all my plans for my novel, all made up out of my head, and I wrote down the names of the characters and the number of chapters and notes about how this was going to be my first book and how I hope it would be a success. It'll be all there for you to see – so the sooner you have it the better.

LARRY   (PAUSE. NOW UNSURE) And that'll be all written in it?

ANN   Of course it will, as you will see, when
             it comes to you, by registered post – and
             maybe then we will get back to some kind of
             normality in this house.

LARRY   Some hope of that and me going to see this
             fellow on Monday.

ANN   (DIRECTLY) And Larry, do you think I'm not
             worried about that too? Do you think I haven't
             seen what's been happening to you and to our
             family these past months?

LARRY   (QUIETLY) ... I'm not saying ...

ANN   Do you not know that it breaks my heart to
             see you ducking and diving and hiding when
             you used to be so different – and do you not
             think that there is nothing I wouldn't do to
             make things better for you and for all of us?

LARRY   (KINDLY, LOVINGLY) I know that, Ann.

             LARRY CROSSES TO HER CHAIR, SITS ON THE
             EDGE AND, TO ANN'S HORROR, PUTS HIS ARM
             AROUND HER BACK, CLOSE TO THE CUSHION, AS:

ANN   And maybe I've been drinking more than I
             should ...

LARRY   I never really noticed ...

ANN   Aisling did! –poor child, how she ever got
             through her Leaving and got her full points I'll
             never know.

LARRY   Well, she's not here, is she? – we ran her out –
             well I did when I ...

ANN   We both did ... and this damn recession
             ...and that budgie thing and the silences,
             everything.

LARRY   She said she'd be back in a year – but to what?
             Where'll we be?

ANN   (QUIETLY) That might not be as bad as we think – Monday. Maybe they'll realise how, before the recession, how good you were, how reliable, and maybe they'll be ... conciliatory.

LARRY   (GENTLY) You always had more hope than I ever had. (RUBS ANN'S BACK – HIS HAND ALMOST ON THE CUSHION)

ANN   (ALMOST FROZEN IN FEAR) Well, we have to, don't we?

LARRY   Yeah. (STANDS) May as well clear up these things ...

ANN   (NOT MOVING) We can do them in the morning.

LARRY   Right. I might head for bed so, if you're coming?

ANN   I'll be up after you. I'm feeling very comfortable in this chair.

LARRY   Right. (TURNS TO GO. THEN STOPS. LIGHTLY) And this book you're writing, from all the stuff in your diary ...

ANN   (ANXIOUSLY) Yes?

LARRY   Will I be in it?

ANN   (WARMLY) You'll be all over it.

LARRY   (RETURNS TO HER CHAIR. SITS ON THE EDGE AGAIN) Good. And when it's finished, I suppose it'll be in the shops and everything and some day you'll all be reading it for your Book Club?

ANN   You know, I somehow can't see that ever happening.

LARRY   Well, I suppose that's something to be thankful for.